The Making of Midge

Mildred Thompson Olson

TEACH Services, Inc.
PUBLISHING
www.TEACHServices.com • (800) 367-1844

Copyright © 2014 TEACH Services, Inc.
ISBN-13: 978-1-47960-444-9 (Paperback)
ISBN-13: 978-1-47960-445-6 (ePub)
ISBN-13: 978-1-47960-446-3 (mobi)
Library of Congress Control Number: 2014951049

Published by

TEACH Services, Inc.
P U B L I S H I N G
www.TEACHServices.com ● (800) 367-1844

Dedication

To my devoted parents: Martin and Margretha Thompson
and my dear siblings: Nels, Dorathy, and Julius
Thompson; Jean Combes; Martina Bakke; Lela Cronk; and
Gladys Ring. I also wish to recognize the members of the
Colman, South Dakota, Adventist Church, who remain in
my fondest memories.

Table of Contents

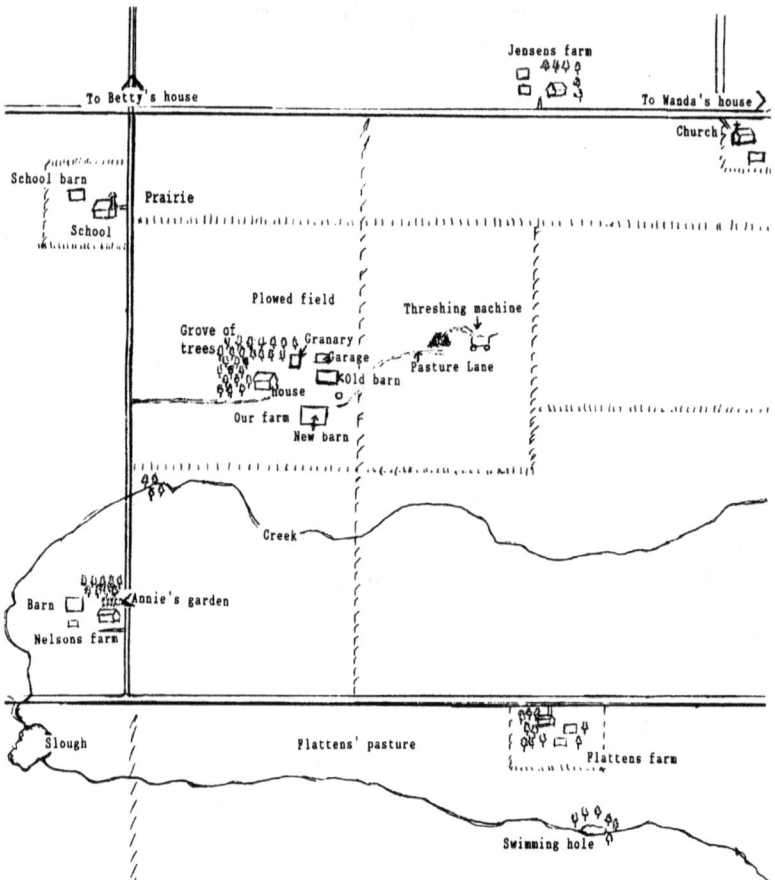

To Betty's house

Jensens farm

To Wanda's house

Church

School barn

School

Prairie

Plowed field

Grove of trees

Granary

Garage

Old barn

Pasture Lane

Threshing machine

House

Our farm

New barn

Creek

Barn

Annie's garden

Nelsons farm

Slough

Flattens' pasture

Flattens farm

Swimming hole

Preface

I always knew that God loved me. I heard it at home, and I heard it at church. I saw God's kind of love practiced by the adult members of the Colman, South Dakota, Church and my family. The stories in this book tell how my parents, my seven brothers and sisters, and the church family led me to choose Christianity and to dedicate my life to God.

I was not the easiest child to raise. I was spirited and mischievous. I pinned wooly tails on guests, I nearly drowned in a flax bin, I set the prairie on fire, and I did enough other capers to earn the nickname, Katzenjammer Kid. Still my family never gave up on me. These pages illustrate how they helped me know that heaven was within my grasp, even when my halo slipped. With each correction, there was encouragement; for every mistake, there was mercy and pardon.

The church family gave me the same comfort and impression—that God was understanding and compassionate. At a very tender age I knew the omnipotent God need not be feared, that He delights in giving good gifts to His children, even to struggling little sinners like me.

In many churches and homes today the children are ignored while the adults indulge themselves in special interests. It was not so in my home and church. The adults didn't just socialize with their peers; they shared time with us. They didn't coddle or patronize us, but they made us know that we were important to them and to God. They modeled Christianity, and we children patterned our lives after them. As a result of their devotion, a surprising number of professional and church workers came from the little Colman church—perhaps more per capita than any other church in our denomination. See the list in Appendix A.

Today there are many one-parent families. The single parent has difficulty in filling the role of both father and mother in respect to the needs of their children. This should be a challenge for the church to stress the importance for adult members to reach out to the children, making them feel loved and needed.

May the stories of my childhood experiences enable parents and church members to visualize the opportunities they have to give supportive care to the lambs of the flock.

The Author

Chapter 1

The Tumor

"I think you have a tumor," Doc Doty said guardedly looking down at the patient lying on his examining table. Then, as he noted the look of horror spread across Mrs. Thompson's face, he added, "But don't worry, Greta, surgery can take care of that nowadays."

"NEVER! I'll die before I submit to surgery" And with that Greta rolled off the table, gathered her clothing modestly in front of her, and waited for the doctor to leave the room. She would not dress in front of a man; her "old country" (for that is the way she referred to her German homeland) morals were still deeply imbedded in her thinking despite 18 years in America.

Though Dr. Doty tried to convince Greta that an early surgery on her tumor, would be advantageous for her, she would have none of it. To her, surgery and hospitals were synonymous with death. "Haven't I seen enough people die of surgeries in the old country?" she snapped contemptuously. "I will not have surgery, and that is final. I'll live as long as God lets me, and then die with my body still whole in my own home. Now, if you will be so kind as to leave the room, I'll dress, pay my bill and go.

The Doctor threw up his hands, shook his head, and left the room. As Greta dressed, she was both frightened and angry. It seemed that bad luck and early death had always plagued her family. Here she was, barely 40, with a diagnosis that she considered fatal. Her Rock-of-Gibraltar courage threatened to crumble as she thought of the seven children she would leave behind. They had brought her such joy that she had almost been able to forget her own miserable childhood.

She dried her tears on a dainty, hand-embroidered handkerchief, placed last summer's straw hat over her swept-up, tightly-pinned bun, assumed a fatalistic attitude, and marched stoically into the reception room.

"Thank you. Here's your fee." She slapped a dollar bill down on the doctor's desk without looking at him. Then she headed for the stairs.

The doctor hurried after her. "No use arguing with a stubborn old German, I don't suppose, but I want you to know, surgeries are successful now days. There's a good surgeon down in Dells Rapids; he can..." It was no use. Greta was scurrying down the squeaky, wooden stairs of the doctor's office, located above the grocery store of their small town.

When she reached the sidewalk, her steps lagged with her drooping spirits. It was early June, and the sweet fragrance of white clover perfumed the air, but Greta was too numb with shock to notice. Halfway down the one-block business section of Main Street, Greta saw the newly painted bench in front of the bank. She slumped dejectedly onto it. "I'll just wait here for Martin," she mumbled to herself. "Wonder what he'll say when he hears that I've got a tumor." She glanced up and down the block at all the familiar landmarks—Bunker's Hardware, Barnes Grocery, Jarrett's Drug, the pool hall, the popcorn stand, the post office, and, yes, the funeral parlor. "Humph! I wonder how long it will be before they have to pick me up for burial," she sighed, a tear escaping her eye. "Oh, Lord,

I don't want to die yet. I love my life here in this quiet community—my country neighbors, the 423 people of this little town, my husband and children, and my church. My years in America have been good—except for the past month when I've felt so miserably sick. I wonder how much worse I will get before the tumor does whatever." She wanted to bury herself in pity with a good cry, but pride kept her from releasing her emotions in public—someone may discover that she, Greta, had a breaking point, too.

Fortunately, Martin drove up just then in their 1917, seven-passenger Studebaker touring sedan. As she stepped off the curb to join him, she was so absorbed with her health that she failed to remember how grateful she usually felt about this modern conveyance. Four years ago they depended upon their horse-drawn wagon for transportation—quite a contrast in comfort and speed to the Studebaker.

"Well, what did Doc Doty say?" Martin asked solicitously as Greta scrambled up on the running board and slid onto the seat beside him.

"That I have a tumor and need surgery. I'm not going to have it, and don't argue with me 'cause that's final."

Martin turned pale. "Oh, no! We must do something about it. If Doc says you need surgery, let's do...."

"NO! Let's go home. Right now!! I hope Martena has watered the baby chicks. It looks as if it might rain, and I need to make sure they get..."

"Greta! For all that's rotten in Denmark! How can you think of baby chicks at a time like this? You should have let me go to the doctor with you. Now, I'm going to stop the car and go talk to Doc myself."

"WAIT! Have you forgotten how hard it is to crank this machine to get it going again? I have several months to think about it. I will be the one to decide WHEN and IF I have this surgery."

Martin had never seen his wife so resolute. She hadn't given him a chance to say anything and obviously didn't intend to, either. It surprised and frightened him, so he acquiesced to Greta's wishes. During the three and a half mile drive home, he glanced at her frequently. Greta was non-communicative, sitting with her jaw set and lips pursed. He knew she would bear her illness with more fortitude than anyone. Her tragic childhood had developed in Greta an almost fatalistic attitude. But he loved her and hoped that she would grasp any chance she might have to live. She was a wise and loving mother and wife; she tolerated no foolishness, rudeness, selfishness, or laziness in her children. She contended that sickness was, for the most part, akin to laziness. And laziness was, in essence, all of the seven deadly sins combined. So Martin, knowing of Greta's attitude about sickness, held his peace and hoped she would bring up the subject again when she was in a more reasonable mood.

Almost three months passed. Martin's patience was wearing thin and his concern haunted him every day. Then, one morning as they were sitting at the breakfast table after the children had been sent to do their chores, Greta volunteered, "You know, Martin, the tumor is growing. I think it's a baby."

Martin nearly dropped his slice of bread and jam into his breakfast postum. "What? Greta this is no time for joking! Didn't the doctor tell you that your child bearing years were past because of, ah,..."

"I know, and I believed him. However, as this tumor grows, I think I feel movement like the movement of a fourth-month pregnancy. Much as I know we don't need another child, I'd take a baby over a tumor any day."

Martin was stunned! "Greta, I hope for all the world that you are right, and that this is not just wishful thinking on your part." He paused, then smiled with relief as he contemplated the alternative. "What do you mean, 'we don't need another child'? We can always make room for one more."

Time confirmed Greta's diagnosis. Her pregnancy was a blessed relief to all. The three oldest children, now in their teens, were almost embarrassed that their "aging parents" were having more children. However, of the two evils, they definitely preferred their mother having a baby over risking surgery.

Summer and harvest passed. Gladys had her third birthday in September; the new baby would arrive in January, so it was time to prepare Gladys for the little intruder who would take her place in the cradle. Then where could they sleep Gladys? The four older girls filled the two double beds in the big south bedroom upstairs. The smaller north bedroom housed the boys. They couldn't risk putting Gladys in with her 80-year-old grandmother because her respiratory problems needed night-time surveillance. Martin struck on a bright idea. During the cool autumn months he built a trundle bed that would slide under their big four-poster in the daytime. When he completed the project, he brought it in for Gladys' approval. She fell in love with her white bed and insisted upon immediate occupancy.

The Making of Midge

So Gladys was prepared to accept the new baby; Lela couldn't wait for the real live doll to arrive; Julius was too occupied with his dogs, calves and school to care about another baby; and 12-year-old Martena was told that, since her petite frame precluded her doing the heavier chores, she would be given charge of the new-comer. Jennie and Dorathy were already high school debutantes and would naturally be leaving home soon anyway, so they weren't that concerned. Nels, however, was already out of school and had remained at home to work on the family the farm. For him, a new baby was quite another story!

Chapter 2

The Child Is Born

Nels, the fun-loving, eternal optimist, was not in a happy frame of mind. He knew very well why he was told to hustle his five sisters and Julius off to church on Sabbath afternoon, January 14. He didn't like the reason one bit. "I hope the folks stop having kids before I get married," he grumbled to Dorathy as he wrapped buffalo robes around his sisters huddled on bales of straw in the horse-drawn sled.

"Why is Mama sick?" Gladys asked innocently. "Don't ask stupid questions," Nels snapped as he slapped the reins of the horses. The team trotted briskly down the snow-covered road. "Just stay covered, or the wind will freeze your breath."

"Why didn't Papa take us to church?" Gladys persisted. "More dumb questions," Nels growled.

"Oh, Nels, be civil. She's only three and a half. She doesn't understand." Sixteen-year-old Dorathy cuddled her youngest sister closer to her. "Papa is staying with Mama because—well, when we get home from church there'll be a nice surprise waiting for you."

Now anyone with any experience in child psychology knows that promising a three-year-old a surprise just before you want her to settle into a quiet church mood is in for trouble. For the next two hours Gladys badgered Dorathy about the surprise, making Dorathy wish that either she or Gladys was deaf and dumb.

About 5 p.m. the seven Thompson children drew into the farmyard. Papa was waiting, "Hey, kids, you got a new baby sister."

Everyone yelled with delight, jumped out of the sled, and ran for the house—everyone, that is, except Nels. His wrath, which had been waxing hot up until this time, now turned to pure steam. "Wouldn't you know it! A GIRL! If there had to be another kid, why couldn't it have been a boy—someone to help Dad in the fields when I leave home. I guess I should have prayed it would be a boy!"

Julius was at the kitchen door when Nels yelled, "Julius, you get back here and help me put this team in the barn." Ten-year-old Julius obeyed that tone of voice pronto. Since Nels was the oldest, he had to assume the "boss" role at times. He usually was lots of fun, but today he was a bear.

Inside the house the five sisters gathered around the hard-coal heater and looked down into Papa's boot box. "There she is," Papa said proudly, pulling back the blanket. He put his rough farmer's finger into his baby's diminutive hand. Instinctively her little fingers curled around his, capturing Papa's heart. "Isn't she a little midget? Just 18 inches long. Shall we name her Midget?"

"No, Papa," Dorathy protested. "We'll think of something better." Then the big girls took turns holding their new sister until it was time for them to prepare supper (that's what the evening meal is called on a South Dakota farm). Their departure gave Lela and Gladys free access to me, the baby. Somehow I survived the pummeling, hugs, and sloppy kisses from the two who were to become my closest friends. Perhaps my 80-year-old grandmother rescued me from annihilation more often than I will ever know.

16

When Nels and Julius came in to change from their church clothes to their chore clothes, Julius sneaked a peak at me. Nels grabbed him, "Come on, Julius, we've got to milk the cows, feed the calves, and check on the sheep. And, oh, yes, you girls, you mother hens, have you forgotten to gather the eggs and feed and water the chickens?" This remark was meant to be either funny or sarcastic, but no one cared. Martena volunteered for chicken duty.

Soon the chores were done and the family gathered for supper. When Nels drew his chair up to the table, he came within five feet of the boot box, but he never looked at me.

After supper Papa and Mama called Nels into the bedroom. "Nels, we are sorry that you are unhappy about the new baby. But she is here, and we aren't going to toss her out. You'll soon learn to love her. She's kind of cute. Take a good look at her, and then you can name her."

Nels finally relented and looked at me. He studied my rosy cheeks and blond hair. In spite of my spastic, newborn motions, a love for me started to grow in his heart, and he chose what he thought was the best name in the world for me. (When I came to years, I tended to disagree with his choice.) He named me Alice, after the missionary daughter of Mrs. Flatten who helped Dr. Doty deliver me, and Mildred, a famous dancer. So I was officially named Alice Mildred. Papa nicknamed me Middy, while the rest of the family called me Midge. And Nels, who played with me a lot, soon became one of my favorite people.

Chapter 3

A Brush
With Death

I was breezing through my first year in good health, needing protection only from Gladys, who claimed me as her dolly. Frequently grandmother rushed to catch me as Gladys pulled me from the cradle, then dropped me. I bounced well and suffered no permanent injuries.

I learned to walk before my first Christmas, so I became a nuisance when they put up the Christmas tree. The ornaments I couldn't break with my hands, I could shake off the tree and smash with my feet. Then there was always the danger of my burning myself on the tree candles when they were lit. In those days the farm homes of South Dakota lacked the luxury of electricity. I think we were the last outpost of civilization to benefit from Thomas Edison's magic wire, switch, and light bulb invention. We had to clip candle holders to the ends of the Christmas tree branches and fill them with little wax candles. I soon learned that flickering flames didn't feel as pretty as they looked.

Water was another big temptation. The Monday before my first birthday, I persisted in being in the kitchen, trouncing around in the wash water that sloshed from mother's hand-operated washing machine. I returned again and again to the cold water in the rinse tubs, spilling water onto my soft shoes and the cold kitchen floor. Mother kept putting me back into the dining room asking Grandmother to "watch Midge."

But Grandmother was in her eighties and wasn't up to hot-footing it after a curious little kid.

The next day, I was a very sick baby. I developed a bad case of pneumonia. That night I gasped short breaths for air. My family took turns holding me upright and praying for my recovery. Nels doted on me, and Martena mothered me, so I willingly took my medicine from these two, my favorite people.

At times like this my family practiced what they believed. They had learned from experience that man's extremity is, indeed, God's opportunity. Whenever we had special burdens, our entire family joined together in prayer sessions. This time their prayer emphasis was for God to save my life. Their prayers were answered by an omniscient God.

Chapter 4

The Katzenjammer Kids

I was less than two years old when I was introduced to my cousin (once removed) and closest neighbor, Leo Nelson. He was about a year older than I so I was enamored with his advanced capabilities. I became a "Leo fan" while still a toddler, and the two of us managed to get ourselves into more trouble than the average kid in the neighborhood. In those days, a comic strip featured "The Katzenjammer Kids"—two children who unwittingly turned ordinary situations into disasters and created havoc by following their wild imaginations. Before either Leo or I could read the funny papers, we were dubbed the Katzenjammer Kids by our families.

One day, for instance, we were crawling on our hands and knees, pretending to be cows. We wanted to get real in our play, so we nibbled the grass. It was awful. Then we chanced to notice Leo's mom's new garden growing just beyond the lawn. The lettuce and onions were already over an inch high. So we moved to Annie's "pasture." We grazed off the onion and lettuce tops. Annie discovered the ravage and cursed the rabbits who she suspected were destroying her garden. A few weeks later, when the lettuce and onions revived, we grazed in her garden some more. When we went in the house for lunch, the onion smell on our breaths betrayed us. The rabbits were scratched from Annie's most wanted list, but we weren't. I left for home suddenly, then, to save Annie the trouble of disciplining me.

It was little things, such as the "cow" episode, that earned us the Katzenjammer Kids reputation. We weren't that different from normal kids, I don't believe; it was just that we got into more trouble in less time, keeping everyone in suspense.

The day we decided we were old enough to handle school, we had nothing malicious in mind. Annie brought Leo up to our house early that morning. Our mothers were going to work together on a project. Our sisters had already left for school, so we were alone to entertain ourselves. We never had a problem doing that for we were creative children. It was the world around us that had problems coping with the results of our activities.

We decided that since we were almost five and six years old it was time we experience higher education. We asked permission to visit school, but Annie laughed derisively, "No teacher in her right mind would want you two Katzenjammer Kids in her school."

Leo and I went outside to discuss that disparaging remark. We agreed that the teacher did want us in school. The more we discussed it, the stronger our convictions grew. Perhaps the teacher was even anxious that we attend school. Besides the pleasure we would give the teacher, his sister Norma, and my sisters, Lela and Gladys, would be most appreciative of our visit. We imagined how much they were missing us at that very moment and how thrilled they would be for us to sit with them in the one-room country school. We would even share our knowledge of gophers, frogs, birds, eggs, and the likes with the other kids. I bragged that the teacher had a special affinity for me. Hadn't she had me sing "Jolly Old Saint Nicholas" for the school program last

Christmas? She even patted me on the head and gave me a bag of candy.

Remembering the candy gave us an added incentive, so Leo and I took flight. We stupidly ran past the screen porch where our mothers were working. Of course, we were caught and interrogated by two experienced mother investigators and were sentenced to stay home.

We made no promises, but our silence was taken by them as consent. We left for the grove of trees north of our house to plan our strategy. We convinced ourselves that we OWED the school our presence. In the pursuit of excellence, we would get to school that day, somehow. We only needed to be more devious.

It was still early in the morning. As we slipped among the trees, we got sidetracked by the swing. Time was an entity of which we had plenty, so why rush? Leo jumped on the swing, pumped himself to a high arc, then sat down on the seat. When the swing died down considerably, Leo demonstrated his courage and agility by leaping from the swing. I responded appropriately to his bravado.

"Of course, you wouldn't dare jump like that you being younger and a GIRL," he boasted.

I hated being younger, and I hated being called a girl. I was always the youngest, and it seemed the older kids used that as an excuse for not letting me do the things they did. And who wanted to be a girl anyway?

"Oh yeah," I shot back. "You just wait and see. My dad is going to get me some overalls, and I'll push my curls up under my straw hat, and no one will know I'm a girl. Besides, I have asked God to change me into a boy. He will too! You'll see! And when I get my overalls on, not even the angels will know that I was once a girl.

My outburst subdued Leo, if only momentarily. "I guess you're right. If the angels can't tell, I s'pose I couldn't. But what will we call you then?"

"Midge, of course. It's a good boy's name."

"O.K., Midge. Get in the swing and I'll push you. Ya wanna try jumpin'?" Leo gave the swing a mighty shove.

When the swing was in its highest arc, I yelled, "O.K., I'm jumping."

Leo paled. "Not ye-e-e-t!" he screamed, but it was too late. I had already leaped from the seat. I landed with a bone-shattering thud on the hard earth. I thought I had killed myself and was very pleased when I discovered I wasn't dead. When I stopped seeing stars, I examined myself to assess the damage. All my bones still functioned, but my teeth seemed slightly loosened. My knees, which had been somewhat protected by my long tan stockings, were scratched and bleeding. My stockings had suffered irreparable damage. They were frayed around the large holes that had been scrapped off in the dirt. The back of my skirt was missing. It had torn off when the hem caught on the swing's board. But I didn't care. I was elated. I had made a most spectacular and daring jump that astonished the socks off Leo. In fact, I recovered from my jump before he did. He was still agape.

When I recouped my equilibrium, I went to the swing, snatched the back of my skirt off the seat, and stuck it in Leo's pocket. Leo finally regained his senses, and managed to say, "Boy, oh, boy! That sure was some jump for a gir…" He stopped when I glared at him. "Ah, for, ah, a little kid." That remark got him in almost as much trouble with me.

"I mean, for a BIG kid. Boy, oh boy! I can't wait for you to get overalls. Then I won't have trouble remembering what you are."

Before we were able to establish any world jumping records, we were distracted by blackbirds swooping down on us. They had become real pests that spring because they pecked to death five to ten baby chicks per day. Our parents didn't like to kill the birds outright so tried to discourage their presence by having us kids destroy their eggs and nests. Leo slipped his leather cap on his head for protection against the bird attacks and climbed the tree. He fished out the eggs and stuck them in his pocket. While sliding to the ground, he accidentally smashed the eggs. The gooey mess stuck all over one side of his overalls.

Now our clothing was in pitiful disarray. My undergarments covered me modestly, even from the back, but no sane mother would have wanted us on public exhibition. Oblivious to our unsightly appearance, however, we headed for the school. We accumulated more dirt by trudging a quarter of a mile though the freshly-plowed field north of our house. When we reached the barbed wire fence separating our land from the prairie across from the school, we crawled through it, snagging our clothing and skin. We were determined little soldiers. We would conquer school that day or give our lives in the attempt.

We thought we were fortunate to reach school in time for their 10:30 a.m. recess. Jubilantly, we called to our sisters. Looks of surprise, then horror, then panic spread across their faces. Rushing at us like maniacs they yelled, "Go home! Get out of here you crazy kids!!"

Go home? No way!! We had risked our all for this day at school.

"Midge, you are a mess! Your dress is torn, your socks are holey, your hair is tangled, and your shoes are covered with mud. GO HOME! NOW!" Lela spit out orders like General Stonewall Jackson.

"Leo, you smell with that gooey stuff all over your pants. You're disgracefully dirty! For SHAME! GO HOME!!" Norma shouted.

Leo and I exchanged glances. We were dismayed by our sisters' reception. We didn't think we looked that bad. Besides, they were always putting us down. How could we trust their judgment now? So we chose to ignore them and stayed.

The teacher came to the door of the school and rang the bell. We filed in with the rest of the kids—at the end of the line. We smiled when we passed the teacher. The look of repulsion on her face escaped us. We ran for desks but were forced out of them by the kids who thought they owned them. Then we discovered that the recitation bench right under the teacher's nose was not occupied. That was more to our liking anyway—front row seats. It was not to the teacher's liking, however. She sent us to the back of the room to share one old junky desk. Then she asked Lela to get a wet rag and wash off the recitation bench where Leo and I had sat. We thought the teacher's pickiness was annoying, but we allowed for her idiosyncrasies.

What really ruffled us good was the way the teacher ignored us or admonished us to "shush" every time we yelled out an interesting tidbit to improve upon her dull educational program.

We talked the situation over. We didn't like being isolated in the back of the room in that dumb old desk. We weren't allowed to divulge the knowledge we had acquired

25

from experience. Maybe the school wasn't ready for us yet. Hopefully, by the time we got to school officially, the school board would have the wisdom to select a more intelligent teacher. We decided that we would return to our world of fun and freedom, and just let that teacher keep her old, stifled ways.

I am sure our sisters sighed with relief when we stole out the door. Besides being disenchanted by the school program, we were getting hungry. With the cold reception everyone at the school had given us, there was little hope that any of them would share their lunch with us.

Our mothers were putting the noon meal on the table when we walked in the door. They gasped when they saw us—as if we were aliens from outer space. "I declare," Annie contended, "I never would have believed that anyone could get as dirty in three hours as you two Katzenjammer Kids!"

"Midge, your dress is ruined," my mother scolded. I pulled the scrap from Leo's pocket and shoved it into her hand. She examined it, turned me around, and shook her head. "No, I can't fix it. Just get a basin of water, go outside, wash, then go change your clothes."

We obeyed, but I heard mother say under her breath, "Honestly, Annie, aren't those kids something! I had seven children—then Midge."

I was pleased with that statement. I considered it a compliment. She had mentioned me by name. A few years later I learned that mother hadn't meant that as a compliment. It was her way of defining the regulars from the impossible.

Annie empathized. "Will they ever amount to anything?"

"Who knows?" Mother sighed. "They surely never lack for ideas. With their energy, they just might do something worthwhile in life."

"But I don't think we'll live long enough to know," Annie said. "Raising them is killing me."

Annie's words of despair were lost on us, but Mom's positive suggestion inspired me. I confided to Leo, "I'm going to be a missionary."

Leo jerked back in astonishment. "Oh, I wouldn't do that if'n I was you. You might get et by canny bulls."

"No I won't," I countered. "Jesus will take care of me."

"Sometimes you are pretty brave for a gi…" Leo stopped, knowing he would be in trouble with me again. "I mean, BRAVE, ah, for a kid."

This would have been a good time to have ended our day, but our gabby sisters came home and tattled on us. We were sentenced to a fate worse than spanking—we were forbidden to play with one another for two weeks. We were to "think how we could avoid getting into trouble."

I thought a lot during those lonely days. I made marvelous resolutions. I determined that I would become a saintly child and make my parents and Jesus proud of me. I'm sure that was the desperate prayer of my parents too. Even though my halo almost always was askew, I felt my family's love and was encouraged that God loved me too.

Chapter 5

Christmases at Our House

My parents made big productions out of every holiday, but Christmases were especially gala affairs. Several weeks before the season, mother prepared every kind of Scandinavian and German pastry and candy that she remembered from the Old Country. These treats were stored away to feed us and the guests we would receive during the two weeks of school vacation.

Having guests and being guests was all very nice, but what our family enjoyed most about the holidays was our time of togetherness. Only necessary work was done; the rest of the time we played together. In the evenings it was table games; during the day it was outdoor fun. Dad and we kids would zip down snow-covered hills on sleds or scoop shovels, or go ice skating on the slough or creek. If the drifts were deep and hard enough, our dad and brothers would dig out igloos big enough for us to crawl into and have our secret powwows with friends. South Dakota winters were so cold the igloos lasted most of the winter.

Besides the delectable cuisine, our family prepared for Christmas in other ways. We usually made gifts for one another since cash was always scarce. Our siblings may not have been too elated with the presents Lela, Gladys, and I so ineptly produced, but they made passable pretensions of delight which made us feel good. Dad's gifts were standard—woolen socks or mittens that he knitted himself during the winter evenings.

Grandmother spun the yarn for Dad's knitting from the wool of our own sheep. Mother purchased combs, ribbons, mirrors, brushes, etc. for us girls and neckties for the boys. Jennie and Dorathy were working away from home by this time, so they usually bought each of us a new article of clothing. Mom invested in a game for the family and a toy for each of us younger ones. As I watched the pile of wrapped presents grow in the corner of the parlor where the Christmas tree would stand, my excitement escalated. I thought I would die of curiosity before Christmas Eve arrived.

On Christmas Eve, the big girls (as we identified my three oldest sisters) would decorate the Christmas tree while mother put the finishing touches on the best of the holiday meals. I vacillated between enjoying the good smells coming from the kitchen and peeking through the keyhole of the parlor door. I was supposed to be helping Lela and Gladys set the table, but since they were doing such a good job without me I set up my spy operations right outside the parlor door. Before I was ready to begin my sleuthing, I heard a funny crying sound from within the parlor. I nearly scalloped myself on the door knob as I hurried to position my eye over the keyhole. I could see nothing but the girls moving about in the lamp light. However, I identified the sound as that of a baby doll crying. Now I had told everyone (not more than 20 times a day, however) that I would be most pleased with just such a gift. Was my fondest wish about to be realized, I wondered? I was tempted to knock on the parlor door and relieve my anxiety by asking my sisters if the sound came from a baby doll. But I knew from previous spy experiences that I would not get a direct answer from them. And I wanted FACTS. I decided that calculated candor might throw Lela off guard and she might blab. It almost worked.

"Did you hear that? That was the cry of a baby doll," I stated positively, trying to conceal my excitement.

"Yes, ah, I mean, what?" Lela stopped dead in her tracks, then turning away from me she added, "Ah, I know. I'll bet that was Santa Claus crying, ah, because he, ah, he burned his finger on a candle."

"Oh, yeah, right," Gladys concurred, looking guilty as sin for conniving with Lela.

I knew they were lying through their teeth. Mother had said there was no Santa Claus. Blessings came from God and gifts from people. I didn't even bother to argue with Lela and Gladys; I knew I would only force them to sin further as they would need to add another lie to the first. So I kept my suppositions to myself.

Then the men came in from doing the barn chores, and our family gathered around a beautifully set table laden with the traditional Christmas Eve favorites—mashed potatoes and gravy, roast chicken, green peas, red beets, white rolls and strawberry preserves. These foods, red, green, and white in color, were chosen because they are the Christmas colors. Then we had candlestick salad half of a banana set in a pineapple ring and topped with whipped cream and a maraschino cherry. Our desert was a Danish specialty—whipped prunes in a buttery, flaky tart, smothered with sweetened whipped cream.

Our mouths watered while Dad said an unnecessarily long blessing, or so I thought; then everyone indulged themselves exceedingly and chattered excessively, while I ate mechanically and dreamed of a baby doll.

After supper there was another agonizing delay for me. The men went out to milk the cows, the older girls cleared the table and washed the dishes, Gladys swept the floor, and Mother and Grandmother rested. I paced the floor.

It seemed like forever before the family assembled again. Then mother held the lamp while Papa lit the candles on the Christmas tree. All other lights were extinguished while we filed into the parlor to get our first glimpse of the decorated tree. Excitement, happiness, and love was reflected in the face of every family member as the flickering light of two dozen candles dispelled the darkness.

I squeezed in to be near the tree. Then my eyes fastened onto the sweetest baby doll ever sitting under the tree! I quivered with longing. I wanted to snatch her in my arms and cuddle the wonder clothed in a soft white bonnet and dress trimmed with pink ribbons. But I knew better than to pick her up. What if she belonged to Lela or Gladys? I couldn't stand to relinquish her. So I waited, but only for a moment. Bless Jennie's heart! She saw the hungry look in my eyes, and relieved my anxiety immediately. "This is yours, Midgy," she said lovingly, handing me the baby doll.

I took the doll with trembling hands and cuddled it ever so gently in my arms. I was euphoric. No gift or other Christmas of my childhood equaled the Christmas of 1927 when I got Baby Bumpkins. Lela and Gladys got dolls in boxes with fancy dresses and hair, but I knew I had the best. Martena had made a layette for my doll, and Dorathy a patchwork quilt. That night, after Dad read the Christmas story and we sang some carols, the happiest little girl in South Dakota fell asleep with Baby Bumpkins wrapped in the doll quilt and the doll clothes stuffed under her pillow. Outside of my Christian family, that doll was my most precious possession.

At earlier Christmases I also had received some special gifts. I still spent hours on my kiddie car, pulling my papier-mache duck on wheels about the house. But now Bumpkins rode on my lap. The kiddie car I called my Whippet (after a new kind of car) and the duck, Ducky Waldo, after Ralph Waldo Emerson. (Not that I knew anything about Emerson, but I thought Waldo was a perfect name for the duck. I heard it from Jennie and Martena when they discussed the literature of this author. Thus I latched onto the name Waldo. I doubt that Emerson would have been flattered by his name sake.)

One night during that Christmas season, my aunt and her family came to our house for supper and games. After the meal, my cousin Emma, Lela, Gladys, and I went into the parlor to enjoy the Christmas tree and tell stories. That night I wanted very much to light the candles.

I begged Lela, who held the box of matches, to let me light just one. She struck the match, and reluctantly handed it to me. I lit the lowest candle within my reach. Then I stretched forward and lit the next highest candle. By doing so I leaned right over the first lit candle and caught my blue velvet dress on fire. However, it was a few seconds before any of us noticed it. Then I smelled smoke and saw the flames creeping up my dress toward my long blond curls.

I ran screaming about the room. Lela and Gladys were immobile with fright. I was about to become a living torch when suddenly Emma sprung from her chair, beat the flames with her bare hands, and rolled me on the carpet. The fire was out, but we were all badly shaken. I owed my life to Emma's quick response. Her hands were slightly burned, and my dress was ruined, but a greater tragedy had been averted.

That night I said a special prayer of thanks.

Chapter 6

Measles, Mumps, and Misery

Leo and I enjoyed many happy hours playing together and making enormous plans for our future—that is, if we survived our childhood. We determined that we would become famous and make South Dakota a household word around the world. But our sisters gave us no encouragement. "You bungle everything you do," they laughed scornfully. For the most part, we had to admit privately that they were right.

There was, for instance, the summer of 1927 when Charles Lindbergh made his solo trans-Atlantic flight. Why, folks in our end of the country raved about his feat as if he were a natural-born Dakotan. During an afternoon conference, Leo and I decided we'd do Lindbergh one better and fly without a plane! We'd give South Dakotans something to really brag about. Birds did it, why couldn't we? How could we know that feathers and hollow bones made all the difference. Even had we known that the ancients had tried the same thing and failed, it probably would not have stopped us from trying. We must have resembled oversized bats with the cardboard fastened from limb to limb across our backs. All of our "flights" from tree limbs or haymow platforms almost ended fatally for us. So we gave it up, realizing that we had no control over something the intelligentsia called gravity.

As we grew older, Leo and I naturally wanted to have more control. We especially would have liked to control our bossy sisters, but we knew they wouldn't relinquish that privilege. Childhood diseases, brought home from school by our sisters, were some of our many "uncontrollables." When the kids at school got the measles, we knew our sisters, probably for spite, would put forth every effort to contract the disease so they could pass it on to us.

One day I got to thinking about the measles. I decided it might be worth getting them so I could brag about "the time I had the measles" as Nels, Dorathy, Jennie, and Martena did. Even as I was hating the way they hyperbolized about something I never had, my turn for experiencing measles was just about to be realized. Already the little viruses were having a progressive party in my veins. Blessed innocent that I was, I anticipated getting the measles with a degree of pleasure.

Then the measles struck—WITH A VENGEANCE!! I got chills, fever, and a stomachache. My head hurt too, and I was miserable. I regretted the day I ever hoped for measles. Now I prayed, "Dear Jesus, if you've got any plans for me, get these bugs before they get me."

My mother, who was my usual source of comfort, added to my misery. She insisted that I must "keep warm so the measles would 'come out of me.'" I sweated, chilled, sweated, and waited. I remembered the demoniacs. Jesus had called the devils to "come out of them." By now I was convinced that the devils coming out of the demoniacs and the measles coming out of me were one and the same thing.

I thought back over my sinful life of five years and concluded that I would probably be so plastered with measles the scabs would have to sit on top of one another. Between fitful naps I peeked at the red, itchy bumps as they "came out" everywhere, hourly. "Jesus," I complained, "I think you have called out more measles than I had evil in me. I really think you should have given Gladys or Lela some of mine." In fact, I had such a marvelous case of measles I was sure evil would never plague me the rest of my life. Jesus had called it all out.

Lela and Gladys were as sick as I was. This comforted me. God knew something about them that I hadn't been sure of until now. They had a lot of bad in them too, that God called out of them. Now I knew why my older siblings bragged about surviving the measles. I hoped I would.

During the next ten days, mother kept the shades pulled in our bedroom to "protect our eyes." We weren't even allowed to read. That was punishment for a Thompson because we loved to read. Martena and Dad came in once in awhile to read stories to us, and that helped some. When we got to feeling better, we played table games together in the bed. Finally, we were released from the dreariness of that dark bedroom. Ten days had never seemed so long. Maybe some day I would want to boast about the time I survived the measles, but for now I wanted to forget them.

When whooping cough started making the rounds at the end of the school year, I knew Gladys and Lela would contract the curse. What pleasures they brought me from school! In fact, I suggested to mother that it would probably be better if I never went to school since diseases incubated there. I appealed to her emotions —I might become a fatality. Mom was unmoved. Then I nudged at practicality—nursing sick kids was wearing her out. "Vell," she contended in the German accent which she never lost, "it's shust as goot dat you get dees tings now— den you von't get dem ven you get to school." How callous could a mother get, I wondered, to think it was "good" that I get sick?

Before school was out the middle of May, the whooping cough caught up with us three girls. We all came down with it at once, but not to the same degree. Gladys became dangerously ill, probably because of her tendency toward respiratory ailments. She lay inert upon the couch in the dining room where someone kept a constant vigil over her. She was ghostly pale, ran a high fever, and drifted into sleep between coughing spasms. Everyone hovered over Gladys. Even the neighbors dropped by frequently with special food or little gifts for her. Of course, our family had regular prayer sessions for Gladys' recovery.

Lela and I felt very sorry for Gladys at first, but then as we became more ill with whooping cough, we began feeling sorry for ourselves. We weren't sick enough to stay in bed, however, and since it was summer, we stayed outdoors, lying around wherever we happened to drop. This was convenient because then we could whoop and vomit wherever we were on the farm. But Mom wasn't there console us. Furthermore, there was no one to give us a drink of water after we finished expectorating. We began to feel neglected and longed for some TLC. We never considered how exhausted mother had become sitting with Gladys and caring for the huge garden alone. And poor Martena! She was nearly run ragged doing all of the chicken chores, laundry, housework, and meals by herself.

One day Annie Jensen came to visit, bringing Gladys a little Chinese lantern filled with candies. That did it!! We were downright jealous now. We were positive that no one cared if we died while we whooped and coughed and turned our innards inside out. The world cared only that Gladys lived. We knew from experience that Gladys always survived her illnesses, so why the big fuss? We craved a little of their attention ourselves—for instance, some candy in a wrapper, if not in a cute little Chinese lantern. BUT NO! Everything was for Gladys—Welch's grape juice, fruits out of season, embroidered hankies, and knick-knacks.

One day I started a whooping spell as we sat on the huge boulders behind the granary. Lela held my head and gave me some comfort. She was a pretty good nurse for a 12-year-old. I was thankful that she did not neglect me as had my sister-mom, Martena.

Then Lela whooped up a windjammer performance. I had no inclination toward the medical profession whatsoever, so I turned aside and gagged a little. I laid on my tummy across the boulder, listening for her to stop her retching. I was relieved when she stopped whooping and started breathing normally—that was a sign she'd be around for awhile longer, alive. We were both so weak we just laid back on the rocks considering our miserable situation.

"Well, Midge, no one knows or cares that we are up here coughing up our toenails," Lela moaned in a melancholy tone that would rival Count Dracula.

I looked down at my bare feet. "My toenails are okay; it's just my stomach that…"

"Oh, I don't mean that literally, you little dummy." (There it was again —I was a dummy). "What I mean is that no one cares what happens to us because we're adopted."

I sat bolt upright. "A—a—adopted?" I squeaked through tightened vocal cords. "You mean like Little Orphan Annie?"

"No, not exactly," Lela continued plaintively. "She was luckier. She got adopted by rich Daddy Warbucks; we got adopted into a poor family—probably for the amount of work they can get out of us."

In my five and a half years, the Thompsons hadn't gotten much work out of me yet. I mulled the situation over in my mind, trying to imagine what my future might be. Perhaps they would make me a household drudge like Cinderella. Up to this point I thought the Thompsons had treated me very well. They read to me and played with me and smothered me with love. I had plenty of yummy food, and I liked my hand-me-down clothes. I thought we were rich, but Lela insinuated that we were with a POOR family. I grew a bit skeptical of Lela's disclosure. "Are you sure we're adopted?" I questioned.

"We must be. Look how they care for Gladys and how they neglect us. We could whoop ourselves to death up here. They probably wouldn't even look for us until the next day. Maybe a week." When Lela's imagination started rolling, she could really paint a graphic scene of our demise.

Soon hot tears were rolling down my cheeks as I pictured the two of us lying dead, side by side, like babes in the woods. We sobbed together as we sat on the stones facing each other, imagining what our funerals would be like. Would they say nice things about us then? Would they still refer to me as a Katzenjammer Kid? Would they be sorry they had neglected us during our final days? Would they weep over our caskets? As these questions came to our minds, we cried all the harder, knowing how sorry they would be THEN.

"Midge! Lela! Come to supper," Martena called from the kitchen door. Her voice never sounded so good to me. I was thankful she interrupted our imaginary funeral before we got buried.

"Come on, Lela," I urged, grabbing her hand. "Let's go for supper. I'm hungry"

"How can you be hungry at a time like this?" she lamented, reluctant to end the period of self-pity she was evidently enjoying. "I'm hungry 'cause I vomited my lunch," I explained practically.

Now who's the one asking dumb questions, I wondered. Stupidity must run in the family.

We wiped our tears on the hems of our dresses and headed for the house—I with more gusto than Lela. She was still harboring resentment toward those whom she thought had mistreated her.

In another week, Lela and I were over our disease. We were able to do our share of the chores again, which gave Mother and Martena a respite from doing everything. Gladys was still very ill, however. Sometimes she turned sort of bluish, which made as fear that we might have to attend a funeral for her. When the chips were down, we knew how much we really loved her and prayed earnestly that God would heal her. The little glass Chinese lantern still stood on the table beside her bed. Not a candy had been touched. That lantern became an omen. I knew when Gladys was well enough to open the lantern, she would live.

Now that we could think sanely again, we realized how terribly ill Gladys really was. Had Lela and I understood that when we were sick ourselves, we would not have been envious of her at all.

Then the wonderful day came when Gladys noticed the Chinese lantern and wanted some candy. I ran up behind the granary and prayed, "Thank you Jesus, for making Gladys well. And, oh, yes, please tell her to share her candy with us."

Gladys did. Lela and I had our share of candy from the Chinese lantern. Basically, I knew that would happen. Our family had been taught to share, and we loved to practice this ethic. And while Gladys regained her strength, Lela and I entertained her by playing table games with her.

Another crisis in the family had passed. All of our family was still alive and able to enjoy one another. I was happy to get back to my church family again to get their words of love and encouragement. Home and church were the places of absolute security and love on earth. In my perfect contentment, I bubbled over with love for everyone and God. I even volunteered Gladys for mission service.

Chapter 7

Living at the Center of the World

Most people didn't know it, but South Dakota was the center of the world. At least that is what I firmly believed until I got into the fourth grade. Then the teacher introduced me to the globe and a geography book, and I made the unnerving discovery that South Dakota was just a speck on what the "knowing adults" called planet earth. I became suspicious of the lot of them. I figured that the globe had probably been made by some alien who out of pure spite or jealousy had minimized the size of my state.

Growing up with seven older siblings had made a skeptic out of me. From my earliest childhood they tricked me and told me fantastic stories. Then, when I fell for their tricks or believed their lies, they called me "gullible," a term which I thought encompassed all of the bad names in English, German, and Danish. Of course, Mother reprimanded them for teasing me, but they managed to pull off some stunts behind her back.

There was, for instance, the time when I was out in the sheep pasture giving the lambs some TLC. Brother Julius approached me with a brownish-colored bar. On his left and right were Aaron and Hur (alias Lela and Gladys) to hold up Moses' (alias Julius) hands. "Here Midge," he said couching his evil intentions in a sweet, mellow voice and angelic facial expression, "I've got a new kind of chocolate bar, and I decided to share this whole plug, ah, I mean, ah, bar with you."

How kind! How generous of him, I thought as I took the bar. I forgave him a thousand trespasses past, and set aside a few future indulgences for sins he might commit against me. The bar looked like chocolate, but the smell and texture belied the genuine. With the confidence born of innocence, I took a generous bite from the smallish bar. Almost immediately my mouth and stomach started a syncopated duet spitting and vomiting. I clutched my throat, "Will I die? WILL I DIE?" I believed that I, like the biblical Joseph, "was hated by my brethren" and that they intended to do me in. I didn't know at the time that Julius had just pulled the same trick on Lela and Gladys and that they had survived the plug of chewing tobacco. Now those two partners-in-crime joined Julius to enjoy some cheap entertainment at my expense. I gave them a fairly good show too. The three of them rolled in the grass, convulsed in laughter, holding onto their abdomens to avoid breaking out hernias. I secretly wished that some wicked witch would give each of them double hernias to be operated on without anesthetic.

After I recovered from the ordeal, we were friends again. I didn't tell mother, though I used the threat of blackmail for several months.

That experience along with a few hundred others caused me to become a peewee skeptic. Now that I was six years old and distrustful of my siblings, cousins, and most adults, I decided to rely upon my own experience and reason to develop concepts. I listened to the "knowledgeables" as they spoke offhandedly of exotic places, peoples, and foods.

I stashed all the information away, sorted it out, and came up with some believable conclusions.

My parents, who had come from Germany and Denmark, said it took six to ten days to cross the ocean. Now I wanted to believe them, but common sense told me that this was not true. Bodies of water weren't that big! I could see across the largest lake in my area of South Dakota; and in ten kid steps, I could cross the creek. No, I wasn't gullible enough to believe that, though it pained me to think that my Christian parents were the ones pandering this misinformation.

Furthermore, no matter what the teachers told the older kids, I knew that California and Florida weren't warm the year around. People visiting us from Iowa and Minnesota, talked about their cold, harsh winters and their muggy, hot summers which were just like ours. Therefore, I must conclude that the rest of the world, what little there was left of it, enjoyed the same four seasons that we did. Of course, the Everglades were covered with snow, and people skated on the Gulf of Mexico in winter. If California grew oranges, they were probably grown in hothouses like mother had for starting her tomato plants. AND that stamp on the oranges that said "Sunkist." Who could believe that? I nearly blinded myself one day staring at the sun trying to detect some kind of lips on that fiery ball. There was no sign of them anywhere. Besides, if there were, how could the sun have time to kiss so many oranges. Then too, why were some called "navel oranges"? Those little indentations in the fruit didn't look like a navel to me.

Those bananas that came in boxes with CABANA printed on them. I figured that they came from the capital of Central America—Cabana. That was the place where all exotic fruit was grown.

What really put smoke in my stack was the geography books that put into print such misleading statements as "Michigan and Washington are known for growing excellent apples." Indeed! I knew that the best crab and pie apples grew right on our South Dakota farm. I had torn many dresses and accumulated numerous scratches climbing the crab apple tree which produced that delicious mid-summer fruit. And our crab apples weren't the puny, cherry-sized imitations that grew in Michigan either. Ours were six bites big, sweet and juicy.

And talking about fruit states—what was wrong with South Dakota? We had rhubarb, wild plums, and goose berries. No one could grow sweeter or larger strawberries than Mom did in her patch. We grew tomatoes, potatoes, onions, radishes, spinach, carrots, corn, and nameless other produce too. Those poor folks living in California had only oranges and bananas, which they probably imported from the capital of Central America, Cabana.

Besides our home-grown foods, we had milk that came from cows and not from bottles, meat on the hoof and not bloody slabs in meat counters, and eggs from chickens and not from boxes. And when we wanted exotic food, we bought them in South Dakota grocery stores which imported those luxuries straight from Cabana.

Yes, I was certainly fortunate to live at the center of the world—South Dakota, where we got 30 degrees below zero in the winters and 100 degrees above zero in the summers. How many places in the world could boast of temperature ranges of 130 degrees?

And something else. We had banks, but they functioned only for adults. Or so I learned one day when I wanted to deposit 37 cents into a checking account. Dad just laughed and patted me on the head, "When you're older, Middy." I wanted to own a check book. Dad, Nels, and Dorathy all had check books. Why not me? I chafed at being low man on the family totem pole, and I determined I'd worm my way up to importance. Someday I'd make them proud and South Dakota famous.

Even though I didn't like the banker, I liked the bank building. I supposed that it was a spot of national interest. There were two Doric pillars on either side of the front with two large windows between. In front of those windows were two wide ledges. On Saturday nights we kids would vie with one another for the ledge space. Those who were fortunate enough to appropriate the ledges for the night could sit and watch the people go by. We knew everyone. The kids of our community would walk up the one and only business block, cross the street, and come down the other side. We repeated this for several hours.

When I first discovered the catbird seat, I had to be lifted up the three feet to the ledge. Then I grew big enough to leap up onto it myself.

It was quite a trick to make the leap without going through the bank window, but I never remember anyone taking the window out.

What we could observe from the ledge made gossip enough to keep our tongues wagging until the next Saturday night. We watched little boys showing off, dashing across the street, hiding behind cars and in dark allies, making nuisances of themselves. We little girls walked around the block, licking on our nickel ice cream cones, nibbling on candy bars or popcorn dripping with country butter. We'd wear our summer's best dresses and hair ribbons, and scream appropriately when a little boy jumped out and scared us silly. But that was part of the excitement one enjoyed growing up in Colman, South Dakota—the center of the world.

Best of all, the city band played on Wednesday nights. They couldn't have competed with the Air Force Band, but our indiscriminate ears didn't know the difference or care. It was gloriously thrilling to watch the uniformed members climb the steps of the bandstand gazebo situated for the summer in the middle of Main Street. Then the high school band director raised his baton, and the music began. We listened to the band and watched the "courtin' age" kids walk the block. Music seemed to inspire them to hold hands, make eyes, and lean against one another for support. Of course, they made us little kids sick, but our repulsion did not keep us from watching them. When we reached our teens, we would apply some of these valuable "courtin' lessons." As a matter of fact, I think we improvised some new ones and improved upon their old techniques.

The place of all places in the world to go was Sioux Falls, a huge city just 33 miles from our farm. About three times a year, my folks would take me there. I'd get so excited about the prospect I could hardly sleep the night before the trip. Folks said New York and Chicago were bigger, but hardly any of them had been there to know, so I doubted the veracity of their statements. Sioux Falls had dime stores filled with toys and all kinds of breakable gadgets from Hong Kong, clothing stores filled with fineries, and bakeries displaying yummy-looking pastries in the windows. I knew that I couldn't have much from any of those stores, but that didn't matter. One day I'd go to heaven which was better and more affordable for me than the stores in Sioux Falls.

There was one fancy store in Sioux Falls that captured my imagination. It was a three-story department store with an elevator. I loved to ride that convenience and thought God could use an oversize version of it to transport the saints to heaven. I think Mom was enamored with the store too. Every time we went to Sioux Falls she would think of some excuse to go to Fantles. I was glad she did, even though we all knew she couldn't afford to buy anything there. I'd beat Mom through the door and then manage about ten trips on that fantastic elevator.

Something even more intriguing about Fantles was the front revolving door. One day Mom left me at the entrance of the store, assuming my sisters would keep me in tow. Lela and Gladys wandered off to interests of their own, leaving me free to investigate the door. I got in the revolving door and started racing around and around in it. I was having a marvelous time, oblivious to anyone or anything. Then Lela suddenly appeared out of nowhere, grabbed a section of the flying door, and pulled me out. I protested her interference with my fun until I saw a very haggard, heavy-set, red-faced lady dripping with perspiration limp out of another section of that revolving door.

"Wh-who," she gasped, trying to catch her breath while she straightened her hat and fur piece, "would turn a child like that (puff) loose on the public? (gasp) That, that urchin has been (puff) racing me around in that door for ten minutes. (gasp) I couldn't run fast enough to get out. (puff) She caught my heels and nearly made me fall. (gasp)

If I had the strength, I'd lambast her!" The lady swooned into the nearest chair and fanned herself. Her eyes bulged as she gasped for air.

Lela attempted an apology and hurried me away before either she or the lady lost control. They agreed a punishment was in order. The mean look in the lady's eyes made me prefer to take my chances with Lela. I was glad to get to the third floor where Mom was looking at patterns. When she heard Lela's story, we left the store abruptly. Back at the car, Mom swatted me several times on the leg and demanded an explanation for my behavior.

"I was just having fun. I didn't even know she was there," I answered honestly.

That night Lela entertained the family with an elaborate description of my revolving door prisoner. My brothers thought it was hilariously funny, but Mom never cracked a smile as she said, "She'd better not try that again." But I couldn't give up the sport. After that I just made certain I was alone in the door.

One summer my secure world was shattered. My parents took off for the Black Hills to celebrate their 25th wedding anniversary and left us kids at home to manage the farm. I saw no reason why I, at least, couldn't have gone with them. I wasn't needed on the farm. I was afraid my parents had left me for good. I missed them so much that I could hardly eat or sleep. My older siblings alternately scolded and pampered me in order that they might keep me alive until my parents returned.

I asked Jennie why it took ten days to go to western South Dakota.

"It's over 400 miles, Midge," she explained, as she cuddled me in her lap.

But that was not good news to me at all. The distance she mentioned was incomprehensible. I knew South Dakota was big. But 400 miles? My parents had gone to the ends of the earth and would probably not be able to return, I feared. Columbus was most likely wrong about the earth being round, anyway. I hadn't seen any "roundness" in the area about me—a radius of 50 miles. So perhaps my parents had come to the end of the earth's surface and were even now tumbling off the edge into never-never land. I prayed that God would catch them and put them back on the banks of South Dakota. I had complete confidence in God's power, and believing that He would return my parents to me was my only source of comfort.

I was never so happy and relieved as the night my parents returned home. They brought me a beaded Indian bag and a nail file that had "Black Hills of South Dakota" imprinted upon it. But the picture postcards they brought back disturbed me just a little. I had always imagined that it would be me who would have to make South Dakota famous. Not so. Gutzon Borglum had already made himself and South Dakota famous by beginning in 1927 to chisel the heads of four presidents in the granite walls of Mt. Rushmore. His feat was so tremendous that in my wildest imagination I couldn't think of anything I could do that would out-famous him. So I had to forgive Gutzon for snatching the laurels from me. South Dakota was now famous, and I was relieved of that responsibility.

Back row: Gladys, Nels, Jeannie, Julius, Dorathy
Front row: Lela, Dad, Midge, Mom, Martena

Chapter 8

Readin' and 'Ritin' and 'Rithmetic

Mother didn't seem terribly anxious to send me off to school, but the fall of my sixth year she roused me from bed, dressed me in a clean cotton print, combed my hair into long curls and tied them back with a red, satin ribbon. While she was doing my hair, she lectured: "Now, Midge, don't talk during school. Answer only the questions the teacher asks you. Don't tear your dress or ride on other kids' horses. Don't climb trees or get onto the roof of the barn. Stay within the two acres of school yard. Don't run off with Leo anywhere. Come directly home after school with Lela and Gladys."

I hoped my brain would retain all those orders. I did want to make a good impression on the teacher since I had failed to do so the year before. Fortunately, the school board had hired a new teacher, so now I could begin fresh.

Mother had purchased real lunch pails for us girls that fall. Most of the kids just carried their lunches in tin, corn-syrup pails.

We had only a quarter of a mile to walk to the square, wooden school house. We usually waited at the end of our driveway for Leo and Norma, who lived just a quarter of a mile beyond us. Then the five of us would socialize as we leisurely walked the stretch together. The other kids rode horses or walked as much as three miles.

Kluge School was better than most of the country schools in that it had indoor toilets, though no water or electricity. It also had a full basement where we could play when the weather was inclement. There were separate cloak rooms for the girls and boys. The large classroom had a bank of windows all across the west wall. The children with poor eyesight, such as my sister Gladys, were given seats by the windows. In South Dakota the sun shines nearly every day, so the light was almost always adequate for the rest of us seated on the far side of the room. A well with a pump supplied the water which we carried into the room and emptied into a large crock with a spigot. We all drank from the same, battered tin cup. Germs didn't have a chance with us tough farm kids.

The first morning of school, the teacher assigned each of us a desk that fit our size. When we had put our new crayons, pencils, tablets, and erasers away, she dinged her little bell and called the roll. The Croons, Flattens, Kruegers, Nelsons, Scrivens, and others answered in their turn. Then she called "Alice Thompson." I looked around. I thought I knew all of the kids at school. Then, "Mildred Thompson." That sounded very familiar, but mother had said not to talk in school unless the teacher asked me a question. I wasn't positive I was being questioned. "Isn't Alice Mildred Thompson here?" the teacher asked patiently.

"Say 'Here,' you dummy. That's you, Midge," Lela said in a course whisper that could be heard throughout the room.

I answered then, but Lela had humiliated me by calling me a dummy. I would have to think of some way to get even with her.

I wasn't good at holding grudges at all, so long before school was out I had forgotten my altercation with Lela. But then on the way home from school Leo's sister, Norma, and my sisters, Lela and Gladys, walked close together whispering secrets. This irritated us because we wanted to know what they were talking about. They got uppity and pushed us away. We ran home ahead of them and got permission for us Thompson girls to go to Nelsons place until five o'clock. There again our sisters treated Leo and I disdainfully. They climbed a tree and ignored us. "Tell us your secrets," we begged from below. Of course, they refused, and this inspired us Katzenjammer Kids to plot revenge.

We went to the barn to discuss ideas. Suddenly our eyes were drawn to the sheep dip spray can. "Let's spray them with sheep dip," we said almost simultaneously. We could hardly handle the five-gallon can and its contents, so we got the red wagon and loaded our ammunition into it. We pulled up to our target as quietly as possible. Then I pumped while Leo aimed the nozzle at our sisters. Norma got one good blast, and, fortunately for me, my sisters got only a few drops. We did stop their gossip session—pronto! The girls dropped from the tree and ran. Our equipment was too cumbersome to follow their retreat, so we wheeled the can back to the barn. It seemed like only a few minutes before we heard Annie yelling, "You two Katzenjammer Kids come to the house—this instant."

We knew our sisters had told on us and we were in trouble. Of course, we could hardly deny their complaint Norma smelled strongly of creosote. Probably the stuff would be hard to get out of her clothing. We hadn't thought of that, naturally, because their cup of iniquity had run over as far as we were concerned. They had been working up to this point with us for the past two weeks. We had forgiven and forgotten the other times, but this time we acted.

Annie didn't see it our way at first, but we finally persuaded her that Lela, Gladys, and Norma were always putting us down and tantalizing us beyond endurance. For once, Annie exonerated us. All five of us made promises and apologies. Then we had some of Annie's spritz cookies and lemonade, and we Thompson sisters went home.

Before I started school, I already knew how to read, write, count, add, and subtract. Lela, who always wanted to play school, had taught me. Perhaps my head start was more of a tribute to her persistence than my intelligence. So to keep me busy, the teacher had me teach the other first-graders what I knew. When I grew weary of tutoring, we younger kids were turned outside to play. These long recesses were the best part of school. I especially enjoyed playing with the two girls who were near my age. Betty Flatten was in my grade, and Wanda Scriven was just two years older. We three girls were also in church together. On Saturday nights, we often stayed in one another's homes. It was nice to have girls to play dolls with since Leo wouldn't and my sisters were beyond that stage. Mother thought Betty and Wanda had a more civil influence on me than Leo. Probably Annie was relieved when I wasn't around to inspire Leo either.

One of my favorite pieces of school playground equipment was the giant stride—a contraption that looked like a Maypole with six long chains hanging from a revolving wheel on top. At the end of each chain was a hang-swing. During recesses or before and after school, I would grab onto a swing and run around the pole until centrifugal force lifted me up and out into the air. It made me feel like an aerial circus performer.

One morning before school I was flying high when a link in my chain broke. I flew free-flight style into the air, then dropped to the ground headfirst. Gladys, who saw me fall, ran to me and rolled me over. Blood trickled across my face from the place in my forehead where a triangular stone was embedded. She called the teacher who took a wet cloth and mopped the sand and gravel from my scratched face. In doing so she dislodged the stone. Then blood spurted out in earnest. I think some of the boys fainted, and the teacher retreated. But Gladys put pressure on my head with a rag, and soon the blood stopped. The teacher asked Gladys to take me home, but I wouldn't go. Big Jim and Annie Jensen had invited me to spend that night with them, and I wasn't going to miss that social engagement.

I stayed at school for the rest of the day and nursed my headache. I didn't know then how deeply the stone had penetrated my skull. That night I walked with Wanda in the opposite direction from my home to the Jensen's. As I walked, I became more ill, but I made the mile and half to Jensen's farm. Annie gave me some Danish butter cookies and some cold milk which somewhat revived me. I rested then until supper. When Big Jim noticed that I only sampled my food, he decided to take me home. Gladys had informed my parents of my injury, but they were shocked when they actually saw me. I don't think they expected it to be more than a deep scratch.

Mother sponged some more dirt and gravel out of the ugly hole with peroxide—her cure-all. Mom never rushed us off to a doctor unless the injury was purely beyond her expertise. In this case, she reasoned that a doctor couldn't fill in the hole, so why bother him? So she cleansed the wound frequently and kept it bandaged. She wouldn't let me go back to Jensens nor school the next few days. (In time the hole did fill in somewhat and healed over. I still bear a small scar and indentation in my forehead from this accident).

When mother asked me why I hadn't come home immediately, I hedged, "I'm going to be a missionary, and they have to be brave." (The real reason I didn't go home was that I was a socialite and didn't want to lose out on an overnight invitation.)

Then mother kissed me on the cheek and said, "But missionaries have to care for themselves when they have accidents."

Dear, sweet mother. She never knew how many accidents we had that went unreported, nor how dangerously we kids lived. We hung from the windmill and tree limbs by our heels. We waxed shingles took them to the top of our long granary roof, sat down on them, and then whipped down to the very edge of the roof before putting down our bare feet to stop our flight. We never once flew off into space. Sending us to school was probably the safest thing our parents did for us. At least we were confined part of the day.

Country kids in a one-room school have certain advantages. They listen and learn from the older kids as they recite their lessons and then relearn them when they reach that stage in their educational program. I reinforced that learning further by playing school with my dolls when I got home. I made workbooks and filled them in for the dolls. Then Lela, like the county superintendent, came around and inspected my work. "I'm going to be a missionary teacher," I confided to her one day.

"That's good, Midge. Maybe I will too."

"But there isn't a Lela missionary," I argued. "My first name is Alice, and there is an Alice Flatten Christensen missionary, you know." "So! Maybe I will be the first Lela missionary."

But one day at school, I caught Lela doing something that I thought brought disrepute upon our church and would eliminate her from the missionary profession for good. A month after school started, the big boys at school decided that they should learn to smoke. Lela and Norma were invited to join them in the barn for this activity. When they locked the barn door and wouldn't let us younger kids in, we spied on them through a knothole we punched in the back wall. There we watched the older kids smoke corn silk wrapped in newspaper.

I was stunned by Lela's participation. None of our family smoked—ever. "Lela's not going to be a missionary," I informed Gladys. "She's going to hell; I can tell you that. SMOKING! Do you think I should tell on her and the Scriven boys in the next testimony meeting at church?"

"Don't you even think it, Midge!" Gladys clapped a hand over my mouth. "I have to go to school with those big boys until they graduate. Love me enough to shut up! Now forget what you saw and quit peeking through that hole."

So I was forced to carry around this dark secret that I was dying to share with my parents and my church. I savored my secret, thinking it might come in handy some day for blackmail. But I never got to use it, and I wasn't even good at keeping secrets. Had I told my church family, they probably would have talked plainly to the offenders and explained to them the unhealthful effects of smoking. Further, they would remind the kids that there would be no cigarette butts on the streets of gold. Though my church family would be sorry that the kids slipped, they would encircle the offenders with arms of love. They would assure them that God still loved them and so did they. The church members' charitable attitude made us want to please them and God.

My education began in a one-room country school where I learned the three R's. I learned a lot of other things too from the twenty or more kids. Gradually I learned what ideas and habits I should adopt and what I should discard. For the time being, I was just occupied with finishing the requirements of grade school.

Chapter 9

In the Good Ol' Summertime

I was all set to enjoy the summer of my seventh year. I had found first grade boring and school confining. By May I was so weary of sitting quietly in school that I gazed out of the windows and longed for the freedom to climb trees, catch gophers, explore the prairies, and frolic with the lambs. During the winter we had built snow forts and igloos with the big kids and sledded and ice-skated during recess. Now all we younger kids could do was swing, jump rope, or watch the big kids play softball. I didn't like watching. I was a participator, not a spectator.

Since my parents wouldn't let me skip first grade, the teacher gave me the run of the library, which was pretty mediocre. I read all of the books through twice or more. I loved listening to the big kids' geography and history classes. What excited me most was studying the globe and imagining where I would end up as a missionary someday. I figured the center of Africa would be a pretty good place. It didn't look too far from South Dakota to me— just half way around the globe. I figured I could spend the holidays with my parents and get fattened up on Mom's good cooking. Then Lela had to throw a damper on my enthusiasm, "Africa is a LOOOOONG way from South Dakota—maybe a month or two by ship." I scorned her uneducated comment. She hadn't been away from the center of the world, South Dakota, either, so what did she know?

Summer began well. As usual, Lela and Gladys organized an early summer picnic for the neighborhood kids. And, as usual, they had it down in Flatten's pasture where a wide spot in the creek made a good swimming hole. My sisters hitched up the horse to the old buggy and loaded up jugs of lemonade and country cookin'. When we passed other kids' farms, we'd stop. Then those children would put their food in our buggy and either walk along behind or ride their horses. It was a happy procession of farm kids and horses that wended their way down the dirt roads, through the pasture gate, and on to Flatten's creek. Kids came from other directions too. There were usually 16 to 20 of us. Now that I think of it, Lela was a pretty brave 14-year-old girl to take upon herself the responsibility of such a mixed multitude of reckless kids.

As soon as we arrived, the big boys together with Gladys and Norma hitched up a rope swing to a willow tree limb. They tied a gunny sack bag full of straw to the end. Then we took turns grasping the rope, wrapping our legs around the sack, leaping off the high back wheel of the buggy, and swinging off into space right over the creek.

Next we tried playing ball in the pasture, but the tall spring grass hid the ball, and the batter could easily get a home run while we hunted for it. We played Indians— hiding behind brush and tree trunks and ambushing one another. If a Blackfoot Indian got caught, he had to join the Sioux tribe and vice versa.

We were starved by the time Lela called, "Food." That was the main event of the day anyway. We soon emptied bowls of potato salad, navy beans simmered in tomatoes and brown sugar, cheese and egg salad sandwiches and apple pie. Lela hid all of the cookies and half of the

lemonade for our afternoon snack. Then she told us stories
for about an hour—the length of time we needed to wait
until we could go in swimming. She said if we went in too
early we'd get stomach cramps and drown. This may have
been true in theory, but we could hardly "drown" in our
swimming hole which was little more than two feet deep.

At last the hour was up and Lela released us to splash
away in the muddy water as if we had good sense. We
sank ankle deep in the squashy mud, and as we stirred it
about with our feet the water became thicker. But it was
wet and cool, and we thought we were having a marvelous
time. The boys wore cut-off overalls, and we girls stuffed
old short dresses into our bloomers.

Before we had had enough of aquatics, Wanda ran
crying to Lela, "I'm bleeding on my arm." Lela investigated.
She sprinkled salt on the bloodsucker and pulled that
culprit and three others off of Wanda. I wasn't good at
watching Lela practice medicine. It made me sick to
my stomach. I asked Gladys to check me out. She found
only one bloodsucker at the base of my skull, and with a
sprinkle of salt she removed the offender. I imagined that
there must be some pain connected with it since there was
blood, but try as I would I couldn't develop a pain. No way,
however, was I going back into that water for an encore.
So I put on dry clothes and enjoyed the sun. But Lela had
to have one last dip, so she flung herself enthusiastically
into the water. The older boys, not willing to be outdone by
a girl, followed suit. They had to prove they weren't afraid
of bloodsuckers either.

By this time it was mid-afternoon. We little kids
played tag as the sun continued to turn us shrimp pink.
Suddenly we heard the lowing of cattle. We looked up

to see Flattens herd of registered Herefords, heads held high, moving purposefully toward us. Perhaps the cattle were only curious about us intruders or were coming to the creek to quench their thirst or some other bona fide bovine reason. But I began having misgivings when they were close enough for me to see the horns on the yearling bulls. Six-year-old Harold Flatten sent the rest of us little kids into a frenzy of fear when he yelled, "The cattle are going to stampede us." We panicked and all tried to climb into the buggy at once for protection. We screamed for the cattle to go away as we crunched one another in the limited confines of one buggy seat and the small truck bed behind it. The big boys laughed at our fears, but as the cattle kept coming doggedly toward us their jeers turned a bit squeaky, and their eyes searched for tree limbs that afforded easy access.

Just when the tension had reached detonation point, Lela let out a yell that surely would have brought down the walls of Jericho. All of the big boys, together with June, Gladys, and Norma flew out of the water like spouts from a whale—everyone yelling in terror (though no one but Lela knew why). The lead cattle, who were almost upon us picnickers by now, snorted in alarm, swung around, and raced the other way, jostling one another in their anxiety to escape the screaming apparitions at the creek. Thanks to Lela, the cattle stampeded—but away from us.

Lela on the creek's bank continued to yell, "Somebody help me!" She kept pulling at the seat of her bathing suit. Gladys and Norma ran to her rescue. Under the privacy of a blanket, they helped Lela out of her bathing suit, and pulled two disturbed crabs from the cushioned part of her anatomy where they were firmly latched. Lela lost some skin, a little blood, and all of her sense of humor.

Everyone had had enough excitement for one day and was ready to go home. Lela brought out the cookies and lemonade. We polished off the refreshments hastily, said our good-byes, and took off for home to do farm chores and nurse sunburns. It had been a marvelous picnic.

We were still peeling off layers of burned skin when Grandmother, who had been ailing the past three months took a turn for the worse. Grim rumors about her dying circulated around the family, but I didn't believe she would actually do it. Grandmother would live forever with us, just like she always had. None of us could remember a day when Grandmother hadn't been around to help in the house, rock us to sleep, or keep us in line. When the older kids went off to school, Grandmother entertained me with her work. I watched her process wool from the raw fleece to the finished product. First, she washed the wool in lye soap and hot water. Then she dried it in the sun, carded it, spun the tags into yarn, and dyed it. The last step was knitting the yarn into mittens or half socks for us. "Shtore-bought vool, no goot," she informed me. I admitted that store-bought wool wasn't as scratchy as hers, so her homespun stuff must be better. She didn't understand what I said, but she accepted my nod as an affirmation and smiled appreciatively.

I liked the yarn balls she made by winding tags of wool into a sphere. Then she sewed pretty designs from yarn onto the ball for a cover. Wool yarn balls bounced very well and never hurt if they hit people. I didn't like Grandmother's pinching us when we made her nervous by playing with the balls on the stairway. She was the world's mightiest pincher. She would grab an arm, pull a piece of flesh between her forefinger and thumb, and twist it. Her pinch left a purplish spot on our arms for a week. We still played ball on the steps, however. Lela, Gladys, and I simply learned to scoot up the stairs fast when we heard her shuffling our way. We knew she would never come up the stairs after us. And since her wrath was short-lived and her memory poor, we knew it was safe to come out of hiding in about 11 minutes.

The day was June 21. Mother was on the phone calling my father's sisters. "Besta-mooer von't last long. Come now," Mother advised them. Shortly the house was swarming with relatives and friends. The ladies fixed sandwiches, cookies, and nectarade (a drink made from a fruit-flavored syrup Mom bought from the Watkins man). While they ate, the adults spoke in solemn, muffled tones. I knew something serious was wrong, but as usual I had difficulty in getting the facts from anyone.

I searched for Lela. She would give it to me straight. She did, "Grandmother is dying—any minute now." That was too straight and abbreviated for me. While I tried to absorb this information, I clamored for more. "Why?" I asked.

"Why!?! Because she is old and sick."

"How old?" I needed to know in order to determine if she was justified in dying.

"Eighty-six and a half."

"Methuselah was older. He was over 900, and that's more than 86." My education had not been in vain. I knew comparisons.

"Oh, Midge, you ask too many questions. Run along. I'm feeling sad." Lela gave me a little shove off the couch to let me know the conversation was ended.

I turned to Gladys. She shook her head. The 10 year old had no desire to tangle with my insatiable curiosity.

Lela and Annie Jensen went into grandmother's bedroom and I padded along behind them. I climbed onto the railing at the foot of grandmother's bed to get a good look at someone "almost as old as Methuselah." Her face was ashen, her eyes closed, and I knew she was sleeping. Suddenly she let out a big sigh and made a funny noise deep in her throat. "Why is grandmother gurgling?" I asked.

No one heard me. Annie Jensen ran from the room, and mother swept in. She felt grandmother's wrist and neck, put a mirror to her mouth and nose, then paused. She said evenly, "There's no sign of pulse or breath."

What a flurry of excitement ensued in the next few minutes. Dad called the doctor and the undertaker, and everyone was crying except me. Aunt Stina came into the bedroom and laid out her "burying cloths." I was bewildered so I crept into an obscure corner to watch the strange proceedings. The word "dead" kept reoccurring in the grown-ups conversation. But I couldn't accept that. Our dog Fido had died, but he was an animal. People couldn't die—God made them from clay. And clay couldn't die, I reasoned to myself.

The doctor wrote out the death certificate, and the undertakers carried Grandmother out to their long, shiny car with curtains.

"Wait," I said, tugging on the man's shirt. "Where are you taking Grandmother?"

"To the morgue to get her ready for burial," he answered apathetically.

Now I was disturbed. No one tried to stop the men from taking Grandmother away. I knew she was only sleeping. I was angry and frustrated so I went back into Grandmother's bedroom and laid down on the foot of her bed to think. But before I got my mind in gear, overly zealous neighbor ladies invaded the room with buckets of Lysol suds and a determination to exterminate any tenacious germ. "Move out of here, Midge. We'll have to fumigate the room. Your grandmother had T.B., you know." I hadn't known that, and I didn't even know what T.B. was—maybe toothbrush? Grandmother didn't have a toothbrush because she was toothless. But I got out of their way.

The next day we went to see Grandmother lying in a gray, velvet-covered box with a satin lining. I pulled a chair over and climbed up to look at her. She looked better than when they took her, I thought, but she was still asleep.

Thursday we went to the Methodist Church, which was larger than our country church, for her funeral. I was glad when they opened the lid—I hated the dark and figured it was just too scary inside that box for Grandmother. When the preacher sat down, they closed the lid again, put her box in the long black car, and drove off to the cemetery with her. I was beside myself with fear when they lowered the casket into the ground. I became hysterical when they began throwing dirt on it.

"Papa, please stop them," I cried. "Just because Grandmother is sleeping so hard is no reason why they should put her into the ground and throw dirt on her. She'll never be able to get out of there now!"

My father turned to me, his eyes full of tears, but he didn't stop them. "I'll talk to you later, Middy," he said. I wanted to pursue the matter further, but one of my sisters led me off to the car. I was too emotionally exhausted to fight the human death experience anymore. So I sat motionless in the car, my thoughts tumbling in confusion. My known world was no longer secure. If I fell soundly asleep for several days would they put me in the ground? Although Lela had talked of our dying from whooping cough and of our funerals, the reality of it all had filtered through my brain like a sieve. This was my first experience with human death, and no one had prepared me for it. Perhaps few adults realize how traumatic the finality of death can seem to a 7-year-old child. Of course, I had heard about death, but it was a mystery to me. It wasn't like I had imagined. It was just like an animal dying, and God hadn't formed animals of clay like He did man! That should make a difference, I thought.

Later that night, Dad cuddled me on his lap and tried to explain what death meant to a Christian. "Middy," he began slowly, "God made man from dust... "

"Clay," I corrected. "Clay holds together better than mud."

"All right, clay," he conceded, not wanting to tackle eschatology with a 7 year old just then. "But clay will break down into dust when it is old. Grandmother was like an old clay vessel—chipped, cracked and wearing away. When she died, her breath left her, and she is returning to dust. She will stay in the ground until Jesus returns. Then, just like the potter can make a new, better vessel from new clay, Jesus will make a new, better, prettier, and healthy grandmother. We can stand beside her grave and watch her burst from her tomb, and she'll look brand-new young. Her hair will be blond again, she won't wear glasses, and she will run with you and..."

"Grandmother RUN? She never ran! Will she still gum her food, or will God give her teeth like yours that come out at night?"

"No, we'll both get permanent, pearly white teeth. Grandmother will be able to run with you. She was tired, and Jesus let her fall asleep."

"Asleep?" I questioned anxiously. "If she's asleep, she can't be dead." I was still having trouble with adults referring to death as a sleep.

"Oh, Middy," Dad sighed tiredly, "we say sleep, but that's just an expression. God calls death a sleep because when you sleep, you don't know anything until you awake in the morning. Right?"

"I dream," I said.

"Child, you are a stickler for words." Exasperation edged Dad's voice. "All right. Grandmother died. But she doesn't hear or feel or know anything at all now!"

"You sure?"

"Yes, Middy, the Bible says so in Ecclesiastes 9, 1 Corinthians 15, and 1 Thessalonians 4 and lots of other places. The Bible is very clear about death. No one can misunderstand it—people die, are buried, and stay in the grave knowing nothing until Jesus returns the second time. Then they are resurrected and taken to heaven with the righteous who are alive at that time."

I comprehended a little. "That's good. Then when grandmother is resurrected. I'll have to tell her about my missionary work because she won't know."

"RIGHT!" Dad agreed, obviously relieved that my interrogation was over. "So why don't you hurry on to bed so you can grow up fast and become a missionary. Grandmother would like that."

I planted a kiss on Papa's leathery cheek, slid off his lap, and went to Mother. She studied my Sabbath School lesson with me and listened to my prayers. When I asked Jesus to help me to grow up to be a good girl, I'm sure Mother added, "And please let it begin now."

Then I kissed Mom, climbed into Gladys' trundle bed, and fell asleep—not dead.

Chapter 10

Wedding Bells Bring Changes

Hospitality was a part of our family's creed. Every member was on the social committee. We loved sharing our fun, food, and faith. Almost always there were feet under our dinner table that did not belong to a Thompson.

Therefore, I became a socialite both by heredity and environment. I loved having visitors—anytime, anyone, any reason. When Martena and Jennie brought their boyfriends home for the Christmas holiday, I naturally assumed the hostess role. Everyone else in the family, however, seemed to want to usurp my job—especially Jennie and Martena. Gladys and Lela accepted our sisters taking charge more graciously than I did. Lela, in fact, purposely steered me away from the foursome, leaving them free to pursue the business of love without being hampered by my presence (and/or curiosity). She inveigled me into playing games with her and Gladys. But I wanted to play games with the guests. One day I decided it was finally time for me to assert myself.

The four lovers were sitting around a card table playing dominos, having a glorious time paying more attention to each other than the game. So I, in an attempt to restore some dignity to the game of dominos and to satisfy my hosting instincts which had been ignored for five days, volunteered to play with them. Gladys wanted in too. She suggested that the two of us could improve the quality of their playing skills and the game. They just laughed, refused our overtures, and continued to ignore us. We felt ostracized. We wandered off to Mom's bedroom to consider their imprudence. The presence of Bill and Marvin had turned our sisters' brains into mush; and, for two schoolteachers, the men didn't seem to have any solids there either. Furthermore, our sisters had selectively chosen the company of the men over us—their own flesh and blood. Whoever said that "blood runs thicker than water" hadn't tested the love potion.

Gladys and I sat glumly on our folk's bed, folding and unfolding our hands. Suddenly my attention was drawn to a box containing hunks of fluffy, carded wool about eighteen inches long and four inches in diameter. (These were carded, raw wool pieces, not woolen yarn.) "Look, Gladys, don't those hunks look like real sheep's tails?" I asked. "Sure do!" she laughed.

"Let's pin wooly tails on Bill and Marvin. That'll teach those love bugs not to be so uppity," I suggested with a sudden spurt of inspiration. "Would you dare?" Gladys giggled.

"Sure," I answered without hesitation—still the Katzenjammer Kid acting on impulse rather than astute judgment.

"I'll get two big safety pins," Gladys said. "You do the pinning." "Okay," I agreed.

Armed with our ammunition, we crept back into the dining room. Gladys relaxed on the couch to watch the proceedings.

I crawled up behind Bill, maneuvered my hands between the spokes of his chair, and pinned the tail to his pants. Then I joined Gladys on the couch. We had to smother our laughter with sofa pillows. Every time Bill moved, the fuzzy wool tail wiggled with his body. It looked exactly as if it grew right out of a hole in his pants.

Now I couldn't wait to give Marvin his tail too. I pushed the safety pin though the wool piece and slithered up behind Marvin's chair. With both hands through the spokes, I tried to push the pin into the seat of his pants. But the pin was rusty and caught on the material. I knew I couldn't stay there very long without being detected, so I became overly zealous and gave the pin a mighty shove. The pin lost; I won. OH, HOW I WON! The pin went through the material, his skin, his flesh, and stopped at the bone. The stab of my injection sent Marvin into orbit with the tail hanging on tenaciously. Marvin upset the card table, and dominos flew everywhere. I, the culprit, was pounced upon; Gladys, my accomplice, rolled on the couch convulsing with laughter.

By the time Mother arrived on the scene, everyone was laughing hysterically as Bill and Marvin pranced about displaying their floppy tails. Since one and all seemed to be enjoying the humorous effect, including Mother, she could hardly punish me. But Mother—conscientious, child-training mother—pulled me aside into the next room.

"Midge, just leave your sisters and their boyfriends alone. Next time you won't get off so easy!! Next time I will punish you!! DO YOU HEAR?"

I heard. It was hard not to! My ear drums were vibrating!! When Mother felt the infraction was not quite deserving of a slap, she talked loud and squeezed my arm hard.

I resolved to make certain reforms, or be more devious the next time. I was fortunate that Bill and Marvin were so tolerant of me and never held any grudges. Our family was to see more of those men, so maintaining a cordial relationship was important.

The Fourth of July, with our traditional church picnic in the daytime and public fireworks at night, was the high point of the summer. All other events paled in comparison, I thought, until one day in August of my seventh year. Bill Combes had come back to our house, accompanied by his parents. They seemed to bring with them an aura of excitement that animated our entire household. I couldn't detect the reason for this inordinate exuberance. I grilled Mother. She only smiled and shrugged, "Bill is sweet on Jennie." Whatever that meant. Did he dab her with sweet stuff like jelly when I wasn't watching? And believe me, I watched! Curiosity was my strongest trait—common sense trailed a long way behind. Whenever I heard something puzzling, I went about like a professional sleuth trying to uncover the truth for myself. If I interrogated my siblings, they'd avoid the issue by saying something like, "We get tired of answering your million dumb questions."

When I saw Bill take Jennie by the hand and lead her into the parlor, I followed at a discreet distance. I took my position behind the door where I had an unobstructed view of the proceedings. They were so preoccupied that they didn't see or hear me sneak in. My eyeballs were riveted on the couple as they sat on the leather divan— real close. I watched with bated breath as Bill slipped his arm around Jennie's shoulders. I rose higher from my blind when I heard her giggle and Bill laugh. He kissed her on the cheek, and I sucked in my breath. The nerve of that westerner! He wasn't family!! Then he kissed her on the lips!!! I gasped aloud in horror. I couldn't suppress it. Martena had just taught me about the germ theory, so I understood what had just happened—Bill had spread his microbes all over my sister's lips. "PHEW! WHY?" I exploded, exposing myself. The lovers glanced in the direction of the sound.

"Midge, you nosey little kid, you get out of here this instant!!" Jennie thundered. She sprung from her seat and moved menacingly toward me. I fled from the house to the safety of the green apple tree branches.

I had to show up sooner or later, however, or starve to death. When I did, Mother was on hand to deliver her lecture in her normal German dialect, "Midge, you yust stay avay from yer sisters ven der boyfriends ist here. You understand?" I understood but I didn't want to follow that advice. I allowed temptation to overpower me many times after that. I knew I was always in danger of detection when I spied on my sisters, but the hours of entertainment I enjoyed while watching the courting process was well worth the risk.

Even with the risks I had taken that summer, however, I hadn't uncovered a clue as to why the Combes had descended upon us. I knew it wasn't for work the harvest was over. I asked Nels.

"They came for the dog days of August, Midge," Nels laughed. "If a dog is going to get rabies, he'll do so during the hot days of August. Then if he bites you, you'll foam at the mouth and choke to death." That was gruesome, I thought. And I couldn't see what that had to do with Bill.

By now, I was getting pretty fed up with my clan who were withholding information from me. My ultimate threat became, "I hope you get rabies—only stop choking before you die." I didn't want to lose any family member. I just wanted something to happen to them to make them realize how poorly they were satisfying me. I imagined myself the good Samaritan, wiping the foam from their anguished lips and saving their lives. I really liked the wonderful missionary I dreamed of becoming. It was harder to be one in real life.

Besides Bill and his family coming to our farm during the "dog days," there were other curious activities taking place. Mother was busy sewing fancy dresses for just about everyone. She made me the prettiest dress I had ever seen and one just like it for Betty Flatten. When I quizzed her about it, she said, "Vill you yust stand still vile I fit you. And stop being a pesky kid." Now I had grown accustomed to my siblings calling me slanderous names at times, but here my own mother was calling me "pesky," which I suspected was a bad Polish name. I got no information from anyone. Everyone was tight-lipped. When they saw me coming, they changed the conversation. I knew I was the only one being excluded from some deep, dark secret, and I didn't like it.

On Tuesday morning mother called me to the kitchen where she was frosting an enormous cake. As my eyes fastened on that inviting creation and I drooled over the prospect of licking the frosting bowl, Mom told me that Jennie was getting married to Bill on Wednesday afternoon. Then she admonished me to tell no one. I considered that for a spell and then decided that good news, like the gospel, had to be spread. I ran and told everyone, privately, of course, "Jennie is getting married to Bill tomorrow, and she doesn't even know about it yet."

For the next 30 years I heard those words quoted. Whenever anyone was getting married, someone in my family would smirk, "I wonder if they know about it yet."

Tuesday morning we "practiced" for the wedding. Betty had just had a small pox vaccination and was miserable. I asked her if she had been bit by a dog too. She wanted to know why. So I had to explain to her about dog days, rabies, and foaming at the mouth. "Do I have to teach you everything, Betty?" I asked.

"Maybe. But don't. You're making me sicker and scareder." Wednesday afternoon was blistering hot. People packed into the parlor and dining room to watch the ceremony. The overflow crowd peeked from windows and doorways. But my parents and Bill's took the best seats in the house—just a foot behind their children. This gave them a real close-up look of their backs. What I couldn't understand was why my courteous parents took the choice seats instead of offering them to the guests. But then this whole weekend had gotten out of control, so why ask questions. Then Gladys Flatten began playing a wedding march. My sister Dorathy and Martena's friend, Marvin Bakke, led the procession. Betty and I followed dropping flower petals while Bill and Jennie came after us grinding them into the carpet. That seemed like a stupid thing to do—someone would have to clean up that mess, and I was afraid it would be me since I had dropped them.

Betty and I tried to stand still as we had been instructed to do. However, that was nearly impossible on such a hot, August, dog day like this. I considered the good fortune of my dog—lying in the cool dirt on the north side of our house. At that moment I would liked to have exchanged places with him.

I looked up at Bill and Marvin. Perspiration was rolling down their faces and splashing onto their wool suit coats. "Take off your jacket, Bill," I whispered softly. Mother

77

yanked the back of my dress, and I turned around. She shook her head and frowned at me. I knew I'd better be quiet, but I still thought all the fuss in this heat was stupid. I even saw little beads of water on Jennie and Dorathy's faces, and they were dressed as coolly as modesty allowed. I didn't feel sorry for the preacher, Gordon Oss, whose rosy cheeks indicated a dangerous rise in his blood pressure. I figured he could wind down whenever he liked. The rest of us were suffering politely, waiting for him to finish.

Just before I dehydrated and turned into a pillar of salt, I heard the preacher say, "What God hath joined together, let no man put us under. I now pronounce you man and wife."

I came to with a start. Let's back up there a sentence. What did Elder Oss mean: "Let no man put US UNDER." Under WHAT? The ground? How far could I trust preachers? It was a preacher who said Grandmother was asleep in Jesus when he meant dead; then out at the cemetery the preacher grabbed the first clod of dirt and crumbled it onto grandmother's casket—"From dust thou art, unto dust shalt thou return." The preacher was the one most anxious, I thought, to see Grandmother be put under the dirt. Dear me! How did I ever get rooked into this wedding deal, anyway? Did the US include me? Jennie? Bill? This was the first wedding I had ever attended so I was unaware of any danger that might be involved. Oh, me! This was a crazy, scary thing to happen on a wedding day! I surely hoped that no man intended to put US under.

During the closing prayer, I was wondering whether to flee or accept fate. When Elder Oss said, "Amen," I started to take off, but mother held me back until Jennie and Bill got out. Then people started to laugh and clap and throw rice—another mess for those who weren't put under to clean up. Obviously most of the crowd hadn't heard the preacher's threat, or they ignored it.

I decided to hang around for the wedding dinner. No use in being hungry too, while they put us under. What a feast we had! Mother had prepared gallons of food, and the neighbors had augmented that with lots more. I forgot about the agony the preacher had just put me through. With that much delicious food around, I just had to indulge in the pleasure of eating and drinking. I ate enough ice cream, cake, and cookies to turn diabetic.

Jennie and Bill left South Dakota a few days after the wedding for Union College in Nebraska where they would further their college education. We never saw much of Jennie after that just in the summers when she would come home for a month's visit. Dorathy was working in Madison, and she came home only for brief visits once a month. So now our family had been cut in size—Jennie, Dorathy, and Grandmother were all missing.

November 28 was the day of my parent's 25th wedding anniversary. They had already celebrated this event during the summer by taking a trip to the Black Hills. I never expected to hear about their anniversary again. Unbeknown to me, the neighbors and my siblings were planning a surprise celebration for them.

The last Saturday night of November, there was inordinate whispering and sly glances between my siblings. Martena whispered to Nels, "It's so foggy. Do you think that anyone will get here?"

"Here? Where? Who?" I questioned now alerted to the prospect of visitors.

"Oh, for pity sake! Can someone gag that kid until... " Nels' voice trailed off.

Just then a car drove into the yard. Nels dashed out, but returned almost immediately. Mom asked Nels who had come and what they wanted. Nels answered in a most peculiar fashion, I thought. "Oh, it was just Andrew Jorgensen. He wanted a good beating. I gave it to him, and he left."

"That's a dumb answer. I don't believe you," Mother fumed. I was jubilant. My oldest brother was called "dumb," too, and by Mother.

Nels didn't respond. He just went outside, got in his model T, and drove off. What I didn't know was that he was out on our country road lining up the cars of the people who had come for the celebration. Our house was hidden from the road by a grove of evergreens both on the north and the west sides. Besides that, our driveway was very long, so my parents couldn't possibly see any activity out on the main road. Mother was rather peeved at Nels for driving off in that terrible fog. "He'll probably have an accident," she fussed.

Then we heard the blaring of horns. We ran to the windows and watched as a long procession of headlights beamed through the fog and drove into our yard. I was in a tizzy of joy, Mom sat down in shock, and dad beamed with pleasure. People poured from their cars laden with containers of sandwiches, cocoa, coffee, cake, cookies, doughnuts, and almost every Scandinavian dessert ever concocted. We little kids darted like bees in a hive among the adults, playing hide-and-seek and snatching choice bits of food. The feast was followed by a program. Lela,

Gladys, and I sang several songs, including the one the community folks always requested—"Puttin' on the Style."

Then my parents were given gifts of silver. The neighbors had pooled their resources and purchased a set of sterling silverware engraved with the letter "T." Such classic table service seemed almost out of place on our table of chipped dishes gotten with coupons or in boxes of oatmeal. Simple things fitted best with our farm decor. All of our furniture was purchased secondhand at auctions. When Dad brought it home, it didn't look like much, but by the time Mother had scraped, sanded, and varnished it we were the envy of some of my friends. I never thought of us as being poor.

Somewhere along the line, Mother did get a good set of dishes too. Then she enjoyed having guests even more. Over a white, linen tablecloth she lovingly placed her new china and silverware.

The following March sister Martena brought home a lovely beige silk dress. Her eyes sparkled as she hung the dress up in the closet. "In two weeks, Marvin and I are getting married," she told me.

"Will you go away with Marvin like Jennie did with Bill?" I asked anxiously, fearing another separation was in the offing.

"Yes, I'll go to western South Dakota where Marvin is teaching school and live with him. He is lonely out there and misses me."

"I'll miss you more than he does," I countered, feeling the pangs of parting already. Up until this moment, I had liked Marvin. He played the violin and sang a beautiful tenor at our family hymn sings. Now I resented him greatly. I hoped he'd never get to Colman at all. I didn't

81

want him to take Martena away from me. She had been my second mom from the time I was born until she went away to Plainview Academy. It was she who had bathed, dressed, fed, and played with me. She taught me to walk and talk. I didn't think I could survive without her. It had been a nice winter because Martena had been taking teacher's training in Madison and was home on weekends. Now all that would end.

"I planned to take you with me to the mission field," I said in an attempt to get her to cancel her plans. "You'll have to give all that up if you marry Marvin, you know." Then brightening, I added, "But say, you could still wear that new dress on the boat and in the jungle."

Martena chuckled. "No, I don't think so. I'm getting married."

Marvin and Martena had a lovely home wedding without many frills. Dolly (Violet) Scriven (later Mrs. Charles Wittschiebe) was the bridesmaid and my brother Nels was the groomsman. Again the house bulged with relatives, friends, and lots of food. Again Elder Oss closed his sermon with that weird phrase, "What God hath joined together, let no man put us under." But since nothing had happened to anyone the last time, I didn't worry about it anymore.

I did have a complaint about Martena's wedding, however. She didn't have a flower girl. I even volunteered for the job, since it wasn't so hot and I hadn't had to clean up the mess the last time. The fact that there were no flowers growing outside in the March snows was not a good reason. I could have yanked some blossoms off mother's indoor geraniums. But Martena didn't want it. I was offended but licked my wounds on big scoops of home-made ice cream and cake. Then Martena left, and so did the company, and the house seemed mournfully silent.

I finally found a way of coping with my loneliness. I cut pictures of boy and girl children out of the Sears Catalog—a set of males and females that looked like they ranged in age from newborn to 21 years. I lined the paper dolls in a row. I cut out two male and female pictures. I, the preacher, married each couple, ending with the standard, "What God hath joined together, let no man put us under." Then I started each couple with a baby. After a little time, I changed the baby for a picture cutout of a 1-year old. Soon each couple was given a new baby. Each family would eventually end up with three or four children who would marry one of the other couples' children. I performed more marriages in less time than any justice of the peace. By the time I needed to change the original couples for gray-haired granny and grandpa dolls, I would be called for supper and would put away my dolls for another day.

As we sat around the supper table, I looked at the gaps in the family circle where Martena, Jennie, Dorathy, and Grandmother had sat. Sometimes I had to swallow a lump in my throat as a tear escaped my eye. We were a hugging, kissing family who cried over separations. I didn't like the changes. I liked it best when I could see and feel every family member. Mom assured me that in heaven my preferences would be realized. So I looked forward to heaven.

Julius, Gladys, Norma, 15-month-old Midge with little lamb, Grandma, cousin Leon in front of sister Dorathy, Martena and Lela by the Ford Model A car.

Chapter 11

We Lose Our Farm

I always felt secure in the familiar haunts of our 180-acre farm paradise. My parents provided a comfortable home, the necessities of life, and lots of love. All of these basic ingredients for human development and contentment grew out of their absolute love for God and trust in His divine guidance. Teaching Biblical principles is very important; but living them, as my parents did, is the best way for children to "catch religion." That's why eight Thompson children live happy, contented lives and wait for the coming of Jesus or will go to their graves with the Blessed Hope of the resurrection.

Besides the positive influence of my parents on us children, they were highly respected in the community because of their honest, Christian lives. They were good neighbors—always willing to help anyone in need. They kept a neat farm; the buildings were nicely painted, and the fences repaired. The sheep were turned into the farm yard once a week to "mow" down the weeds and grass. We maintained a clean grove of trees by burning the dead wood in the cook stove. Mom's flower beds were admired by everyone, and we girls kept the lawn well manicured with the push mower. Dad was always adding improvements to make our lives easier. For example, he installed a hand pump in the kitchen that brought rainwater in from the cistern. For our large family, this convenience saved us girls many trips to the well. Dad's inventive genius showed up all around the farm with other of his labor-saving devices.

Probably Dad's talents were developed out of necessity. When Dad's parents first moved onto our farm, there was only the old school house building with the lean-to. Dad added to that original structure until the Thompsons now luxuriated in a four-bedroom house, complete with parlor. Through the years he built farm buildings—a large barn, hen house, granary, corn shed, coal shed, buggy shed (in my day it was a garage), wash house, chicken house, and a two-seater outhouse.

Then as motorized equipment and automobiles made their entry onto the western plains, Dad built a new garage with a work pit so that he could stand under his machines to repair them. Yes, Dad was a good mechanic too. In his new garage he put a huge stove with a metal shield around it. Here he could work in the cold winter, repairing machines, harnesses, or saddles. The furnace, aided by bellows, also served as his forge for blacksmithing. If Dad couldn't find the item he needed for repairs, he would beat one out on his anvil.

Dad had a separate tool shed under the granary. Almost no one except Gladys was admitted to this private sanctum. He had a hook on the wall for every implement, and a homemade cabinet with drawers made from wooden Land-O-Lakes, three-pound cheese boxes. In these boxes he kept his nails, bolts, and washers of various sizes.

Leo and I liked to sneak into Dad's tool shed to do some inventing of our own. One day dad came upon us by surprise. We were pounding on the fuse of a stick of dynamite, not knowing what it was. "Here, you kids," Dad yelled, startling us nearly to death. "You want to blow yourselves to bits?" He shoved us out the door saying, "Now you two stay out of here unless I send you in here for something. I won't lock you out because my faith that you will obey me should be lock enough. Christian's honor?" We nodded, feeling most fortunate that Dad wasn't big on spankings now that he was older.

By the close of World War I, my older brothers and sisters were doing the farm work. Dad rented more land to earn more money to care for the needs of his expanding family. By growing more fodder, he could raise more livestock. Cattle needed shelter from the harsh Dakota winters. Therefore, Dad borrowed money from the Colman Bank and built a huge, super-modern barn. This proved to be a fatal mistake—building at a time when lumber was very expensive. During the next ten years, farm prices plummeted, interest rates soared, and crops were poor. Then came the stock market crash of 1929 which spelled financial doom for thousands of Americans. Hundreds of people claimed bankruptcy, but dad didn't think that was an honest way of settling his debts. So one day Dad went up to his bank in Colman to see what he could arrange. The bank was closed! Stunned farmers and townspeople mingled in the street discussing their losses. But none of them had lost as much as Dad.

Dad returned home broken. Tears streamed down his sun-tanned cheeks as he told Mother, "Greta, we are going to lose our farm, and e-everything. I've worked these 36 years for this farm. In 1893, when I was a 13-year-old boy fresh from Denmark, I came here. I built and paid for every building on this farm except the shanty that housed us the first few years. I've lost it all! The bank holds the mortgage for only a fraction of what it is worth. I'm so sorry! I don't want you and the children to suffer, but I don't know what I can do." And Dad cried some more.

I crept into the dining room where my parents stood, mutely struggling with deep emotions. I had never seen them so upset. It scared me as I traced the look of pain and hopelessness in their faces. I wanted to comfort them, but I didn't understand the magnitude of their anguish. My parents had always been in control of themselves because they were always in touch with God. Now, however, our security seemed to be at stake, and I wasn't sure how or why or what had happened to my parent's relationship with God. I supposed that He had deserted them if they were going to "lose everything." This was contrary to everything they had taught me, so I was really scared.

With the initial shock past, Mother dried her tears. "Martin, we may lose the farm, but we haven't lost everything. We still have our children and our health and our God. With His help we will start again, and we will keep on living." That was celestial music to my ears. Now I knew we weren't going to die and get put in holes. If Mother said we would go on living, that was gospel to me.

But the bank did foreclose on us and put our farm, the equipment, and the stock that didn't belong to us children up for public auction.

The morning of the sale, almost no one ate breakfast but me. Dad choked back tears all through worship and the rest of the family cried freely. Then we knelt for one of our special family prayer sessions, during which time each one of us prayed aloud. Dad's prayer was very specific. "Lord, this morning we have special needs. You know how I have tried to borrow money from several people in order that I might buy back some of my equipment and stock so that we can make a new start. But no one seems to have money to loan me. The bank is closed permanently. Lord, if in anyway You can manage it and it is Your will, please send me $500—before the sale begins today. Amen."

It was a pretty depressed family that went out to do the morning chores and finish lining things up for the auction. About 10 a.m. the miracle happened. Henry Otter, the husband of one of our church members, drove his team and lumber wagon into our yard. He went to the barn where dad was pitching hay down to the cattle for the last time.

"Hey, Martin," he called, "come down here. I've got a story to tell you."

Dad went down to where Henry stood and listened. "I don't know why, but I tucked away $500 from my last cattle sale. I put it in an old sock under my mattress instead of taking it to the bank. Thank goodness, or I would have lost it in the bank closing. I'd forgotten about that money until this morning when I felt strongly impressed that you need it. I'll loan you this money at no interest if you want it."

Dad couldn't believe his ears. It was a surprising but precise answer to his morning prayers. Tears flooded Dad's eyes as he reached out a trembling hand to take the sock. "Five hundred dollars!" Dad whispered in awe. "Henry, God sent you. I prayed for this exact amount of money—$500—this morning. I really need it and want it to buy back some of my stuff so I can make a new beginning. I will pay you back. I don't know how or when. I don't have a farm after today, but maybe God will provide one I can rent. Three hours ago I had no earthly reason to believe that I'd get $500 either, but I hoped that God would work out something for us, and He has."

Then Henry got a little choked himself. "Well, who'd ever believe God would use me? You know, God's more interested in us than I thought."

Long before 1 p.m., when the sale was to begin, people started swarming onto our place. I was excited as I mingled with the crowd, the hot dog and coffee vendors, and the Lutheran Ladies Aid Society who sold sandwiches and sweets. It seemed that a carnival, without the rides, had come to our farm. Leo arrived, and we ferreted out the main spots of activity. I think we were the only happy people in the whole community. Everyone else was acting as somber as if they were off to an execution of sorts. Leo and I didn't realize that this sale might mean we would no longer be neighbors. The community folks, however, knew that after today the Thompsons would be gone, and this made them sad. Small clusters of men talked quietly among themselves; women dabbed at their eyes. Leo and I couldn't grasp the dichotomy—our pleasure, their sadness.

Then the sale began. Leo and I stood beside dad to watch the bidding. He stood still as a statue, pain masked his face like a tattered veil. He didn't seem conscious of our presence. As one of our well-matched teams of horses was led to the auctioneer, tears filled his eyes. He looked at his $500 and knew he needed to spend it wisely. He couldn't buy back much, just barely enough to start again—if he could rent a farm from someone. Mother came out just briefly; then she fled back to the house, wiping her eyes on her apron. She couldn't stand to see her favorite animals being sold to people. Neighbor ladies tried to comfort Mom; the men tried to bolster Dad. This became a very distressing day for me now. I couldn't bear watching my family suffer.

When the day finally ended, our entire family was drained. As if in a trance, we watched men load up some of our animals and farm equipment and drive away. Now I knew what foreclosure meant; now I felt the loss we were suffering.

Then a beautiful thing happened. We didn't know it at the time, but days before the sale some of our neighbors had formulated a plan to help us. They agreed to bid very low on certain of Dad's best animals and farm equipment. If one of them bid, none of the others would bid against him. If Dad bid, they would all let him have it at his price, and no one would bid against him either. At the time of the sale, Dad had felt a little sad that his best things were going so cheaply. After almost everyone left, these good neighbors led their purchases to Dad. "Well, Martin, where do you want us to put these animals of yours?"

"B-but they aren't mine anymore. You bought them," Dad stammered, not understanding their intent.

"So we did. But we bought them to give back to you. You've been such a good neighbor all these years. You took care of our animals when they were sick. You and your boys have helped us plant and harvest our crops when we were in a bind. Now it's our turn to show our appreciation for what you have done for us by giving back to you some of your best animals. We redeemed them for you, Martin!"

Before Dad could recover from that shock, the banker came forward. "That's right, Martin. We want you to stay in this community too. So I have arranged with the creditors for you to stay right here and rent your own farm and your own land. You won't even have to move—if that's what you'd like."

By the smile on Dad's face, it was evident that was exactly what he wanted. I noticed, though, that dad was hard put to say anything. He just bowed his head and shook hands with his benefactors. They couldn't seem to talk either. They just shook hands, gave a few bear hugs, patted each other on the back, blew their noses, and separated.

With everyone gone, Dad and my brothers went into the barn and milked our redeemed cows, curried our redeemed horses, and closed the door on our redeemed sheep. We ate the food cooked on our own stove around our own table. Before going to bed, my family knelt for another prayer session and thanked our God for good neighbors and miracles greater than we had ever imagined. Peace and contentment reigned once more at the Thompson farm.

Chapter 12

Never Again

The day after the sale my family was adjusting to the losses we had sustained. We were still praising God, however, that it had not been worse. As for me, an innocent of seven, my life was back on track. The Dakota sun was shining, the family was in their usual places at the breakfast table, and we had our standard meal of oatmeal and fruit. After worship we scattered to do our assigned chores. Lela, Gladys, and I quickly finished our tasks so that we could practice acrobatics in the haymow of the new barn. Aerial trapeze work had become a consuming passion with us since the circus had been in town. The trapeze performers embarrassed us farm kids with their skimpy, flashy outfits, and stunned us with their agility at flying through the air. Just as we three future acrobats were headed for the barn, joy of all joys, Leo and Norma appeared on the scene. Now the five of us could perfect our acts, go on the road, and startle people by our daring acts—dressed in more modest apparel, of course. But Dad came along just then and delayed our plans momentarily by asking us to pick up all of the trash left around the place from the sale.

Work was a way of life for farm kids, so we didn't resent the interruption. We knew we would have time to play when the work was done. Quickly the five of us set about the task, and soon the two acres of farm yard was clean. As we picked over the ground, we noticed that smokers had left long butts of cigarettes. These butts became a temptation to all of us, but Leo put it into words. "This is the best time for us to learn to smoke. After all, it won't cost us anything because the butts are plentiful. Besides, smoking will make us grow up faster."

I argued that I was enjoying my childhood and didn't want to pass through it too rapidly. But when Leo promised that it would make me a man, I capitulated. I did want to be a man—above all things. I had even taken to wearing Leo's overalls and tucking my blond curls up under my straw hat. I figured this way I could fool people and the angels until God got around to making the real change. If God could remove mountains, surely he could change one wishful little girl into a boy. I hadn't read Paul's admonition—"In whatever state I am, therewith be content." Except I wasn't content with my female state.

Lela and Norma accepted Leo's plan, but Gladys objected. "It might hurt my lungs," she said. "I've just gotten over a bout with pleurisy."

Lela solved that problem. "Gladys, you don't need to smoke, but promise you won't tell on the rest of us either." Gladys promised. Next Lela persuaded her to go to the house for matches. "Mom will never question you, Gladys. She never suspects you of doing any mischief—just Midge and me."

Gladys agreed and ran to the house. She returned in a few minutes, flashing a box of matches. She grinned, "No one even saw me! No questions asked."

The five of us secluded ourselves in the new barn between the calf pens and the horse stalls. We sat down on some bales of hay. Gladys struck the matches and lit up the cigarette butts for the four of us. We sucked in and blew out like we had seen the "pros" do it. We coughed and sputtered. I was soon so sick I threw down the cigarette and staggered from the barn. My stomach threatened to dismiss my oatmeal, my head was swimming, and my lungs craved clean air. Leo yelled after me, "Stick with it, Midge, or you'll never be a man."

When the earth finally stopped spinning, I flung back an answer as defiantly as I could muster in my miserable condition, "I don't care if I never become a man." I just wanted to be a kid without stomach cramps and a headache. "Oooh," I groaned.

Leo muttered some disparaging remarks about my needing bottles, pacifiers, and the like. I ignored him until the haze had cleared from my brain. Then I whipped out the one word that usually subdued Leo. "I can't smoke, you dummy! Have you forgotten that I'm going to be a MISSIONARY? Missionaries don't smoke!!" I thundered, feeling likc Moses reprimanding the children of Israel at Mount Sinai.

Leo was silenced. Every time I brought up the subject of missionaries, I put fear into his heart. He said it reminded him of church, the Bible, and all of his sins. I took advantage of his holy fear and got the most mileage possible from it. Since he was a year older than I was, he assumed the "boss" role in our partnership, and I resented his acting superior to me. When religion came up, I was swift to reel off judgments, substantiating them with scripture I quoted from my revised, substandard version. After scaring Leo good with a hell fire barrage so hot that it would make the devil cringe, I switched to a pitying, pretentious tone, "Yes, Leo, you have piled up quite a heap of sins for a kid your age, and it will be a struggle for God to know what to do with you. But He will probably forgive you since He is so merciful and good."

My conscience often gave me a bit of trouble with this speech since I was usually a party to his mischief. But Leo was either naive or too concerned about his own future to turn the tables on me.

Soon Norma and Lela were sick enough to join me outside. Further, an incident inside the barn might have encouraged them to end the orgy sooner than planned. A cigarette butt had caught some hay on fire. Luckily the girls were able to stomp it out and save the barn that had caused us to lose our farm. What irony it would have been if that barn had gone up in smoke the day after the farm sale!

We girls had had enough. We never tried smoking again. Unfortunately Leo persisted until he mastered the filthy habit. He died of cancer at age 30.

That night our sin of smoking troubled our consciences. After we Thompson sisters had studied our Sabbath School lesson, we found it hard to say our prayers. Lela, sitting on the edge of the bed, expressed the feelings of all of us, "Midge, I feel real bad about our smoking today. It isn't good for us or pleasing to God. Just last night, after the sale, we were so happy to talk to God because of His big miracles. Tonight I'm ashamed to face Him."

"I know," Gladys agreed. "How could we fall into sin the day after such blessings? I'm glad I didn't smoke like you and Midge."

"Don't need to rub it in," Lela scolded. "I feel bad enough. Sort of like an Israelite at Mt. Sinai hearing God's voice one day and marveling at His majesty, and the next day worshipping the golden calf."

"But we can ask for forgiveness and promise never to do it again, can't we?" I asked anxiously.

"Sure we can." There was a lilt in Lela's voice. "What does Romans 8 say?" We didn't know, so Lela gave us a quick summary. "It says that Satan cannot lay any sin on God's elect—that's us. And no one can separate us from the love of God, not even an angel."

"Wow! So let's pray," Gladys said, dropping to her knees.

It was good to have older sisters who could recall encouraging scriptures just when I felt I had committed the unpardonable sin. I prayed until, in my mind, I could see God's smile of approval and feel the warmth of his love encircle me again. It was only my guilty conscience that had caused me to feel separated from God. He had been there all the time.

Chapter 13

Accident at the Fort

Floyd, a new boy, entered second grade and changed my life. I thought he was about the cutest guy I had ever seen. He had an intriguing lisp. I wanted so much for him to like me that I practiced his manner of speaking until I perfected and adopted it. Mom ignored the new habit I had acquired from Floyd. She thought it had something to do with my losing my front teeth. Then too, since Mom, with her German accent, had trouble saying her "J's" and "W's" correctly, she may not have wanted to be my critic. So when I slurped my "S's" and "Z's" out of the side of my mouth, she made no effort to correct me. The lisp became a serious speech impediment.

During my fifth grade year Lela came home from high school speech class, feeling destined to help me overcome my speech handicap. She sat down in a chair in front of me, made me watch her mouth as she opened it to make the "eh" sound at the beginning of the letter "S," then observe how she closed her teeth to let the air carry the "SSS" ending. She showed me how I did it wrong and how I should do it right. Though my pride was stung because I felt like a baby learning to talk, I finally overcame my problem.

Six years later I won the high school's speaking contest. Lela wrote from college, "Midge, don't you think

I deserve the credit? If I had not forced you to enunciate correctly, you would never have reached first base. Let the school keep the trophy, but send me your medal." I kept my medal and gave Lela my thanks.

As a second-grader, I, like most kids, enjoyed recess more than anything else about school. When the teacher got real busy with the older kids, she let us younger ones out to play if we had our work done and didn't have three marks on the board against our name for talking. Hide-and-seek, tag, pump-pump-pull-away, dare base, swinging, and teeter-tottering were our favorite spring and fall activities. But winters provided the material for the most creative fun—snow! We scooped out igloos in the high drifts, rolled up fat balls for snowmen, built snow forts, played fox-and-geese, and ice-skated in the meadow pond.

Beyond a doubt, the snow forts were the most fun of all. All of us kids, big and little, could play together in the forts. First, we chose up sides. Then each group cut blocks of snow and worked together to build three-foot high barricades. Next we prepared our snow cannon balls, and the battle was on. If a kid was hit with a snow ball, he had to join the side of the enemy. The side that had the most kids at the end of the recess won the battle. Once the snow forts were built, they could stand in place most of the winter with only mild repairs, especially if we'd throw water on them to ice them down.

Because I didn't lie, I was labeled a "tattletale." When anything went wrong, the teacher asked who did it. Of course, no one would say who was guilty. The teacher soon learned to single me out. I would beg her, "Please don't ask me because I don't want to tell." But she persisted, going down her roster, name by name. I could look her in the eye, until she got to the name of the culprit. I said the same thing, "I don't want to tell," but shifting my eyes indicated that she had singled out the transgressor. Then that child would receive some kind of punishment because I had "told." I hated that procedure and wanted to leave school because I didn't like being put on the witness stand all the time.

One day after school, I didn't want to leave with the others. Lyle had gotten into trouble because my reaction to the teacher's question had unveiled him. So I hung around the school door, and Leo hung around too. Not with me, but near me. He wasn't going to let the kids give me any guff. "After all," he pointed out, "Midge can't help herself. She's got to be honest; she's going to be a missionary. Besides, she didn't tell who did it, she just looked it." I was relieved when the kids left for home and didn't wash my face in snow.

After they left, I thanked Leo properly, and we decided to play in the fort for awhile. Our homes were close to school—mine was just a fourth of a mile away, and Leo's a fourth of a mile beyond ours—so we had time before we needed to get home to do our chores. Leo took one fort, and I took the other. The March sun had melted the snow a bit that day, so when we pressed the snow into balls, we noticed they had a tendency to become icy hard. We should have remembered then that was the reason the whole school had not played at the forts that day. But at ages eight and nine, we didn't realize the danger of icy snow balls. Besides, the possibility of either of us hitting the other at that distance was very remote. We were in the best of spirits when we began the attack. I soon used up my supply of snow balls, and neither of us had hit the other. It looked like a draw. Then I bent over to make a few more snow balls. Just as I turned aside, Leo threw a big icy snow ball that hit me just behind the left ear. I fell to the ground, stunned.

When Leo couldn't see me behind the fort, he rushed over to see what I was doing. He knelt beside my limp form, rolled me over on my back, and asked, "Midge, what's wrong?" Leo didn't even know he had hit me. Then he noticed the icy snow ball laying near me, and it scared him nearly to death. He figured he had killed me since I didn't answer him. He ran and got the teacher who was still at school.

When the two of them returned, I was sitting up, still a bit dazed. I had a throbbing pain on the left side of my head and ear, but I was able to walk to the teacher's car. She drove me home.

Mom didn't think my condition was serious—it was just a little snowball, wasn't it? Not being a doctor, she couldn't have known that my ear and the bone behind it were injured. During the next few days she let me stay home from school because I was so lethargic. I laid on the couch in the dining room day and night. The only nourishment I kept down was grape juice and soda crackers.

One night Dad sat by my side, brushing tangled curls from my forehead with his calloused hand. "Middy's hot, Greta," he observed. "We'd better call Doc Doty again. She must have been hit pretty hard by that icy snow ball. I feel an indentation in her head."

I heard what dad said, but I felt so tired it didn't even worry me.

The doctor concluded that I had developed a mastoid problem where the snow ball had hit, causing my skull bone to cave in somewhat. Thelma Scriven, a nurse living near us, came every day and gave me hot fomentations behind my ear. The next two months slipped by without my perceiving the passage of time.

Eventually something must have helped my condition[1] I awoke one day and smelled something that delighted my senses—the lilacs blooming right outside my window. I went to sleep with snow on the ground, and I awakened with the lilacs blooming and summer in the air. School was out, and I was well enough to enjoy the summer.

More than anyone else on earth, I think Leo was the most relieved to see me well again. He had been very depressed over my condition, blaming himself for my illness. But I never blamed him. The accident was a thing neither of us could have anticipated. Leo and I were still the best of friends, and we had the whole summer ahead of us to enjoy. Leo expressed my faith as well as his when he told me, "Midge, I knew you were awfully sick, and for a time I was afraid you might die. But then I remembered God would make you live."

---

1   Later in my life I learned that my mastoid problem had been complicated with rheumatic fever, leaving me with a heart murmur.

Chapter 14

Seasons in
the Country

"To everything there is a season." We Thompson kids would have believed that even if Solomon hadn't recorded this gem in Ecclesiastes 3. We liked every season in South Dakota because each was so different and could, therefore, be filled with so many different activities.

Winter

First came winter with its variety of outdoor fun. Every South Dakota kid knows the fun of building forts and igloos, rolling balls for snowmen, and sledding down hills. But I was especially fond of bobsledding. On moonlit Saturday or Sunday nights, Dad would hitch up a fast team of horses to the bobsled and tie little sleds on behind. Then, just like magic, even before Dad got bells fastened to the horses' harnesses, about fifteen of the neighborhood kids appeared, and we were all set for the best of parties. Half the group stayed at the house and helped Mom fix popcorn, hot chocolate, sandwiches, and walnut fudge. The rest of the group sat in the bobsled on bales of hay covering themselves with buffalo robes. Part of the fun was watching their friends get tipped off the little sleds trailing behind the bobsled. When the sleighing group got cold, Dad swung back past the house, and let them off to get warm, dry, and fed. Then the group in the house layered on clothing and climbed into the bobsled.

Bobsledding was the one activity in which I was allowed to join with the big kids. Gliding along under star-studded skies, moonlight reflecting on the snow making the crystals look like sparkling gems, feeling the brisk air, hearing the bells jingling, young people laughing, and snow crunching under the sled's runners, is a living memory of pleasant feelings, sights, and sounds.

It must have been an immense amount of work and expense for my parents to sponsor this community activity, but I believe their interest in our salvation inspired them to do it. One night I heard Dad tell Mom, "At least we know where our children are—at home having fun."

Ice-skating was another wonderful winter activity. On Sundays Dad would grab his skates and lead his brood down to the slough or creek. We all had skates that fastened to our shoes with clamps and straps. (None of us had heard of shoe skates in those days.) Though all of us became pretty good skaters, none of us could cut figures or skate as gracefully as Dad. He had done it on skates fastened to his wooden shoes when he was a boy in Denmark.

During the week, Lela, Gladys, Norma, Leo, and I often spent an hour after school skating on the creek. One night our sisters were too busy to skate, so Leo and I went without them. We skated further than usual. We followed the creek, going under the bridge and on down into the slough of a neighbor's pasture. Suddenly we realized it was very late. The sun sank quickly in the west, and the moon came up round and bright. Just as we were slipping off our skates, the coyotes started howling. Their eerie cries sent shivers down our spines. Seeing the silhouettes of the coyotes just above us on the hilltops answering each other scared us silly. We whipped off our skates and set a kid's Olympic record in the mile sprint for home. I was completely exhausted as I stumbled in the kitchen door. The family was already eating supper.

As I climbed up onto my chair, Lela asked, "Why are you puffing, Midge?"

"Ran (puff) home (puff)," I mumbled, still trying to catch my breath. "Why? An 8-year-old still scared of the dark?" Gladys smirked. "No," I lied. "Supper (puff), sundown (puff), cold, coyotes (puff)." "You scared of coyotes?" Julius laughed derisively.

"No, just when there's (puff) lots of them (puff)," I said defensively.

Everyone around the table was grinning except my parents. I knew I was going to be teased about being afraid of coyotes. Then my blessed mom came to my rescue.

"You older children just stop right now. You are always telling Midge stories to scare her. You take advantage of her credulity. And there isn't a one of you that wasn't scared of coyotes at her age. But she wasn't around then to be able to taunt you about your fears,"

Then Dad chimed in. "Besides, there is probably not one of you that still wouldn't be frightened if you were surrounded by coyotes. Wolves and coyotes aren't supposed to harm people, but just as I wouldn't tangle with a hungry dog I wouldn't tempt a coyote either. Would any of you?"

My siblings stole silent, embarrassed glances at one another and said never another perverse word. I think they realized that they sometimes teased me more than was fair, and they were sorry. That night each of them seemed anxious to do something nice for me. So I went to bed thinking how lucky I was for such a wonderful family.

On long winter nights we had plenty of time to play table games together. We almost never quarrelled because we understood that sometimes we would win and sometimes we would lose. But if we raised our voices, Mom would sing quietly, "Angry words, oh, let them never, from thy mouth unbridled slip. May the heart's best impulse ever, check them e'er they soil the lip." Or she might take off on "There is beauty all around, when there's love at home." It is amazing how effectively these two songs worked to bring us little "beasties" back into control and remember that we were playing for fun, not blood.

Mom never played with us. She would sit near a kerosene lamp and crochet or darn socks. "It's a good diversion for the rest of you," Mom affirmed, "but I've got better things to do." DARNING SOCKS! A better thing to do? Sometimes we wondered about Mom.

Long winter evenings seemed incomplete without a snack. Mom would make a batch of fudge or maple candy with black walnuts or she'd pop a couple dishpans full of corn, dripping with country butter. There was plenty of free ice in South Dakota from November through April, so winter was ice cream season too. Our two-gallon freezer made just enough for a meal for our family. Mom varied the vanilla flavor with homemade toppings of chocolate, caramel, or strawberries.

As soon as radios came into vogue, Dad got one that ran on batteries. Rural electrification didn't come to our part of South Dakota until 1940. In the 1930s I still had to fill the lamps with kerosene and wash the glass chimneys every day when I got home from school. We enjoyed our battery-operated radio as much as did the city folks who ran their radios on electricity. Our family gathered around the radio cabinet to listen to such programs as "Amos and Andy," "Fibber Magee and Molly," "Orphan Annie," and "Major Bowes Amateur Hour." Of course, Dad never missed the noon farm market report either. And we girls seldom missed a baseball game during the summer. We waited impatiently through winter for summer afternoons when we hoped our favorite teams, the St. Louis Cardinals and New York Yankees, would make the World Series.

We weren't dependent upon the radio for our entertainment, however. With such a large family, we made our own entertainment. Every Friday night we'd lounge around the living room while Dad read stories to us from the Youth's Instructor. I enjoyed those stories so much that I wanted to stay awake for them. However, after a day at school, play in the crisp outdoors, a big supper, and a warm bath, I drifted off with the hypnotic, mellow tone of my father's voice reading the stories.

Most of us girls played the pump organ well enough, but Gladys was definitely the expert. Since there were no piano teachers near us, Gladys enrolled in piano correspondence lessons. She practiced on our old pump organ. By the time she got her diploma for the course, she was playing very well. Our family loved to sing, and that was a hobby we enjoyed anytime, anywhere. We sang when we worked, walked, or rode in the car. But most of all we liked to sing around the organ with Gladys in charge. She had a beautiful soprano voice, Lela had a mellow voice with a wide range, and I had a low voice that naturally made me the alto. When the older kids left home, we three "little girls" (as we were endearingly referred to by our family, since the three older sisters were called the "three big girls") formed the Thompson Sisters Trio. Our voices blended quite well together, and we enjoyed singing specials for church, camp meeting, and our neighbors. Lela played a Hawaiian guitar to accompany us for community gatherings since we couldn't carry the organ with us. We never got any bookings for Broadway, but we enjoyed harmonizing and performing. The community folks always wanted us to sing "Puttin' on the Style," a song that unmasked the artificiality of people pretending to be more than they were. South Dakota country people were forthright folks and expressed their thoughts kindly but honestly, so they enjoyed these provincial songs.

The Dakota winters had a habit of dragging on. About the last of March, after snow had melted and my hopes for spring seemed validated, Mom Nature vexed our spirits by dumping a foot of snow on us. This disgusted me. I didn't like having my spring plans freeze-dried.

Spring

Eventually winter succumbed to spring, and how we enjoyed that season. The farm became a nursery for baby lambs, calves, chicks, and ducklings. Of the 200 or more lambs born on our farm each spring, there would always be some that were orphaned or rejected, especially if a ewe had triplets. Dad carried these little rejects into the house, placed them in a cardboard box near the heating stove, and let us give them bottles of milk. Bottle lambs were the sweetest of all pets. They followed us all over the yard. Whenever we went outside, we had a pet parade following us—two dogs, five cats, three lambs, ducks, and chickens.

I spent time cuddling the soft baby chicks and downy ducks. Usually, sitting hens hatched the duck eggs for us. When the ducklings became mobile, they headed for the pond. The poor mother hen amused us with her frantic efforts to warn her babies of the danger. She knew chicks didn't swim! How could she know that we humans had tricked her into hatching the wrong kind of babies.

Mess time on the farm, Midge helps Dad feeding lambs with bottles.

A big spring event for elementary school children was the Moody County Field Day held in Flandreau. Each school selected their best athlete to compete against other students within the age group. There were long jumps, high jumps, ball throwing, and races of all kinds. I entered them all, but never managed to earn a blue ribbon—a red or white one, maybe, or none at all.

I did much better in the county spelling bees. One spring I made it right up to the finals, and expected to clinch the victory. There were just two of us left standing. I had spelled the most difficult words correctly, and felt confident of winning the laurels for myself and my school. I was given the word "across." I almost smiled; such an easy word! I had victory in the bag! Quickly I spelled it ACCROSS. "Wrong!" shouted the judge, startling me out of my senses. My competitor won, spelling the word correctly with only one "c." I was crushed.

Second prize meant nothing to me; I wanted FIRST PRIZE.

Mom sympathized with me a little, but as usual she was ready to offer some free advice. "Midge, you knew how to spell that word, but you were impatient for the contest to end so you could get the prize. So instead of calmly thinking of the word, you got overly confident." Oh, how well Mom knew me! "Now, if you can just learn to become patient, and think before you rush into things, you'll succeed in your Christian life. Losing a contest isn't fatal, but losing heaven is. So learn something from this experience. Be patient, trust God, and be a winner!"

Summer

I don't know that I had a favorite season, but summers had to rate pretty high. I was free from school and shoes. I hated pulling weeds, but liked the fresh garden produce. I wasn't too fond of watering the chickens and ducks, but I loved watching their antics. Pushing the person-powered lawn mower wasn't my favorite pastime, but romping in the fresh-cut lawn, staining my bare feet green, was exhilarating. And I loved watching Mom's flowers bloom. I think she grew about every kind listed in the seed catalog. Some of those flowers fascinated me because they seemed to have a wisdom of their own. Take for instance, the purplish-blue, bell-shaped morning glories. How did they know they should open only during the morning hours and close before noon? Did those plants have some special communication with God that the other plants didn't enjoy? Sometimes I caught the four-o-clocks jumping their time schedule, but they still seemed to have a better sense of time than we kids. When I grew older, the biology teacher explained this phenomenon to us, but I still liked to think that it was God's manipulation. I spent the summers marveling at the different kinds of plants. In my mind, I thought God started off creation week rather lethargically—light, clouds, air. Then the third day, He really picked up the pace. In a frenzy of creativity he spoke into existence the ground and covered it with thousands of plants. I wondered how He could even reel off the names of so many plants in one day. But He said He did, and I believed Him. Then the fourth day, He relaxed a bit by just doing the sun, moon, and stars. My mind had not yet grasped the extent of that day's labor—the galaxies, revolutions, gravity, etc. On the fifth and sixth days, I believed God was amazingly busy—creating all the animals, birds, and fish, and finishing it off with people. I knew the devil made the flies and mosquitoes, just for spite, to take away some of the pleasures of summer. I looked forward to the time when we wouldn't be plagued with them anymore. Most thrilling, however, was the hope that one day I could stand on the walls of New Jerusalem and watch Jesus recreate the whole earth new.

Camp meeting, coming in early June, was also a wonderful part of summer. At the end of the week's spiritual feast, members were invited to pledge money for the August mission offering. My dad, his faith set in concrete, always pledged a generous amount. And, despite my Mom's concerns, Dad was always able to pay off those pledges. Because Dad had a covenant relationship with God, he didn't take out crop insurance like most farmers did. He claimed he was insured with the bank of heaven, and God always rewarded his simple faith. We never had a complete crop failure, even during the worst drought years. If the corn didn't mature, the oats and flax did. If we didn't get wheat, we got barley. God always gave us something, and we seemed to have more than some of those around us. Besides the lack of rain, there were other destructive forces with which the farmer must contend— cyclones, hail, and insects. We never had a cyclone hit us, but hail sometimes stripped the corn or flattened the grain.

Then came the year of the locust plague. The grasshoppers swept through western South Dakota, devouring everything in their wake, even nibbling on the wooden fence posts. The pests were heading east, so Dad listened every noon to the farm report to learn just how near they were to us. Their progress was steady and relentless. One morning Dad was particularly pensive. After breakfast, the family gathered as usual and listened as Dad read the adult Sabbath School lesson. When he finished, I dropped to my knees, expecting him to pray. But Dad was saying, in a slightly tremulous voice, "Family, we need God to fulfill His promises in Psalms 91 and Malachi 3. The grasshoppers are coming through here today, and unless God intervenes our crops will be lost."

Together we repeated what has become one of my favorite scriptures: "He that dwelleth in the secret place of the Most High, shall abide under the shadow of the Almighty. I will say of my Lord, He is my refuge and my fortress; my God in whom I will trust. For He shall deliver you from the snare of the fowler and from the noisome pestilence." The rest of the family completed the verses, but my mind got stuck on the "noisy pests." My family believed that God would deliver us. I felt God in the room, and opened my eyes to see Him. I was not disappointed when I did not. Our relationship with Him was so intimate that morning, that, like the wind, I did not need to see Him. I felt His presence and was satisfied.

We waited expectantly as the day wore on. During mid-afternoon, a big, dark cloud appeared in the west. It was the grasshoppers! But just before they got to our fields, they lifted and dropped down somewhere to the east of us. Then they disappeared completely. That day a lesson of trust in God and His answer to our prayer was indelibly impressed upon my mind. I still refer back to that memory at times when I need to renew my confidence and hang onto God's promises to His children.

Summers brought long nights of extended light. Dad and we kids stayed outdoors quite late—playing ball, walking on stilts or barrels, or swinging from the gunny-sack swing that let us fly as high as the second-story barn roof. Mom, of course, didn't join us. She preferred "working in the garden when it is cooler." She did go with us to the carnivals but wouldn't ride on the ferris wheel or a roller coaster. She persuaded us not to "waste our money by throwing balls at moving targets." Mom enjoyed the circuses that came to Sioux Falls every few years, but disapproved of the immodest dress of the trapeze artists.

In the summers we made play houses in the grove of trees, marking off the rooms with twine string. Boards over stones became tables and beds, log chunks made our chairs, and overturned calf pails made our cook stoves. Our dolls sat propped up against trees. We made fancy mud pies and decorated them with stones and leaves and dried them in the sun. We had the good sense not to sample any of our creations. The best time came when Mom brought out sugar cookies and lemonade. Then we'd gather in one of our playhouses and enjoy afternoon tea.

Summer meant haying time and harvest. Haying was hard work, but not as demanding as harvest. When the grain was ripe, Nels or Julius would drive the binder through the field, cutting the grain and binding it into bundles. After it dried a few days, we girls set it into shocks of six or eight bundles. This was hard, mean work. Besides straining our muscles to capacity, the beards of the barley and wheat gave us rashes. If I had a choice, I opted to herd the cows along the road to graze down the grass from the ditches. Of course, herding cows wasn't a time for meditation either; Mom sent socks along for us to darn. All other work was set aside when threshing time came. This was a time of accounting for the farmer. When his grain was threshed, he'd know by how many bushels he got to the acre and by what the selling price was how he had fared financially. Harvest time was a most intoxicating season for me since, for once, I was allowed to hang around the men folks. It made me feel like "one of the boys." Lela and Gladys had to stay at the house and help Mom prepare huge amounts of food to feed the 20 or more men threshers. Their voracious appetites paralleled that of Paul Bunyan, I believe. They'd polish off six chickens, five pies, eight quarts of green beans, sixty ears of sweet corn, ten loaves of bread loaded with butter and jam, a peck of potatoes, and gravy. This was just the noon meal. Besides that, they made quick work of all the sandwiches, cookies, and lemonade we served them for afternoon lunch too.

Since my brothers were capable of running the farm, Dad earned extra money on the side by working for other farmers. He sheared sheep in the spring, bailed hay and threshed grain in the summer, and shelled and shredded corn in the fall.

Since Dad owned the threshing machine, he had to solicit threshing jobs from farmers and organize them into crews. Usually there were five or six farmers in a crew. Each provided bundle racks, grain wagons, teams of horses, and men in proportion to his acreage. This was no problem since threshing depended upon community cooperation. Everyone worked every day with the threshing unit until everyone's grain was threshed.

Usually two of the older men were given the easier job of hauling the grain to bins while the young bucks did the more strenuous work of pitching bundles. Nels and Julius each drove bundle racks while Dad kept a constant guard on the thresher which was run by a fly wheel and belt from the tractor. He warned everyone, especially me, to stay away from those moving parts. "It can take an arm right off you, Middy, or pull you into the machine." Dad made no idle threats, so I obeyed. I didn't want to get dismembered or lose my observation rights either.

The days when the threshers came to our farm, I hurried with my chicken chores and carried extra pails of water to the house for cooking so that Mom would have no excuse to keep me from going where the action was. A thrill of excitement shivered up my spine when the young men came whooping into our yard, driving their horses like charioteers. I was not allowed to ride with them or "get in their way." So I waited until Big Jim arrived with his steady old mares, hitched to a grain wagon. Big Jim was a mountain of a man, filled with as much kindness. He always stopped where I waited, reached down a hand and pulled me up onto the seat beside him. He was called "Big Jim" Jensen—330 pounds—to differentiate him from the just plain Jim Jensen—a mere 210-pounder. Big Jim was too heavy to be jumping on and off bundle racks. Even climbing up the wheel to get into the seat of the grain wagon was a big strain on him; so he "hired" me to get water and run errands for him. He often handed me the reins and let me try to drive his horses into just the right spot so that the grain would empty properly from the end gate of the wagon into the elevator.

Jim made me feel needed, and I loved him. I also loved my dog, Amos, and insisted that he ride with us on the grain wagon. Amos went everywhere with me, and I didn't want him to get too hot as he ran along beside the grain wagon. I feared he'd get rabies during the dog days of August. So before we drove anywhere, I jumped down, picked up Amos, and handed him up to Jim to hold while I drove the horses. When we neared the threshing machine, we switched jobs. I finally figured out that he didn't want the other men to see him holding Amos while I drove. Mom told me to keep his secret. For once in my life, I did.

When Jim and I got back to the threshing machine, we usually had to wait for the next grain wagon to fill. That gave me a chance to watch the teams pull the bundle racks alongside the platform where the men pitched the bundles onto the conveyor belt. The bundles moved down into the hopper where they were chopped into pieces. The heavier grain would filter down into a pan where it would be elevated to the grain wagon, while the straw would be blown through a galvanized tube by a fan onto the straw pile. I could never figure out how that machine was so smart. Dad just smiled and said that threshing grain was a gift of mechanical inventions while growing grain was a gift of God. Since I couldn't understand either, I just accepted both by faith.

Sometimes the horses spooked at the rumbling movement of the conveyor belt at the bundle platform. This spelled danger for the young men driving the bundle racks. I watched anxiously as the brave young man lunged for the reins and tried to bring his runaway team under control. I knew that runaway horses had caused the death of more than one farmer in our area, but I was sure it would never happen at our place. Every morning at worship, Dad always prayed for the safety of the threshing crew, and I knew God would answer his prayer. There never was a serious mishap around Dad's rig, though I watched with bated breath a few times when horses ran away.

At the end of each day, Big Jim opened his coin purse and dumped a bunch of change into his hand. "Take just two," he'd say. I fingered through them until I found two dimes. (Gladys had taught me that thin dimes were worth more than fat nickels and copper pennies.) Then Jim would chuckle and give me a nickel and a penny bonus for my "work."

One day Dad was threshing flax on our farm. Flax takes longer to fill the wagon than do most other grains. I got bored waiting around, so I was more than glad when Annie, for some reason, turned Leo loose on us. This meant, of course, that before the afternoon was over we would most likely conjure up some trouble. We did. First of all, we let Big Jim go back up to the field with the grain wagon alone, while we stayed to play in the flax bin. The flax seeds felt cool to our bare feet. The slippery seeds also let us sink gradually deeper into the bin—acting much like quicksand. When we got almost waste deep, we'd reach for the edge of the bin and pull ourselves back out. We laughed as we played, oblivious to any danger. Then I jumped too far into the middle of the bin, and to my horror, I couldn't reach the edge to pull myself out. I sank deeper and deeper as I thrashed about trying to save myself. I panicked and yelled to Leo for help. Leo panicked too when he realized he was not strong enough to pull me out. Just then, with God's perfect timing, my Dad arrived home from the field. He needed some tools from the shed which was located directly under the flax bin. He heard our screams and dashed up the stairs to the bin. He reached out his strong arm and pulled me out. When he set me safely on the walkway between the grain bins his voice was shaky and angry. "Don't you kids know that you can drown in flax? If I hadn't come along just now, it would have happened to you like it did that little boy down near Renner—he sunk to the bottom of the flax bin and smothered. I ought to give you two a good lickin', but I don't have the time right now. Now get out of the granary and stay out."

I had given Dad quite a scare. I know I had had the biggest scare of my life. Sainthood seeped into my soul; even Leo was subdued and felt the need to atone for our stupidity. "Bow your head, Leo, I'm going to pray," I said. When I was certain he had closed his eyes, I said a passionate prayer of gratitude, "Dear God, thanks so much for saving my life. Even though I'm not a very good girl sometimes, I intend to be. And help Leo to become a good kid too. Amen."

I looked up then to see Leo standing reverently like the pictures of Samuel. "You're supposed to say 'amen' after me, Leo, if you mean it." Leo cooperated and mumbled a strained "amen." I was satisfied that I'd gotten some religion into him.

We decided to practice wearing our halos by offering our services to the women. They were greatly bewildered by our saintliness, but they let us fulfill our share of good works by carrying water and wood, feeding the chickens and bottle lambs, and running other errands.

It was nearing the end of the afternoon before the women ran out of errands for us to do. We wandered aimlessly out to the new garage. Here Dad stored barrels of gasoline and oil in the summer and operated his harness-making equipment and forge in the winter. Leo bemoaned the fact that he had never seen the furnace heat the forge. So he suggested that we build a red-hot fire in the furnace and try do a little blacksmithing. We had no particular project in mind, but this seemed like an acceptable activity for two reformers. As usual, our curiosity benumbed our judgment. (If it could ever be said that we had any judgment at all). So we stoked the furnace with paper, grease rags, wood, and coal. What a glorious roaring fire we made! But it was too hot to get near the forge.

Just as we were contemplating our next move, we looked through the garage window and saw Big Jim emptying another load of flax into the elevator. We decided we could accomplish more of our plans if we got a ride with Big Jim backup to the threshing machine. After we enjoyed watching the thresher, we could walk home, checking out our gopher traps on the way. By then the furnace should be cooled down enough for us to do our blacksmithing. We always planned our schedule so that we could pack in the most activities possible. Big Jim agreed to give us a ride and held the horses while we climbed up onto the wheel and tumbled into the wagon box.

While we watched the flax fill the grain wagon, we kept on the lookout for Dad. We'd rather he didn't see us. As we let the grain cascade through our fingers, we chanced to look down the slope toward our farm buildings. We caught our breath in alarm; black smoke was belching from the new garage. "Oh, my goodness, the garage is on fire," Leo cried.

We raced the sixth of a mile home, sensing the real danger if the gasoline barrels would explode and send balls of fire to the other farm buildings. I cried and prayed as I ran, "Oh, please, Jesus, save the farm. And forgive me for goofing again."

Leo gave instructions as he ran. "Go to barn (huff), get calf pails (puff), fill with water (huff) from horse tank (puff), throw in furnace."

We did just that. Of course, the cold water cracked the cast iron belly of the furnace, but not beyond repair. Fortunately, the garage was not on fire. The smoke was coming only from the chimney, and the fire had spread only to some papers and gunny sacks in front of the furnace, but it was on its way to the gasoline barrels.

Wonder of all wonders, no one else had seen the smoke. It was visible from the threshing area so we couldn't understand why no one else had seen it. Thankfully, another calamity had been averted. A few months later, Dad discovered the cracked furnace. He couldn't figure out how that could have happened. I volunteered no information.

We were dog-tired as we sat on the big stones on the shady side of the granary. We looked across at the new garage, still standing securely. We discussed the afternoon's events. Had all of this taken place in just three hours? We had been more fortunate than we deserved that afternoon. So we resolved to make some real reforms.

We were almost model children for two weeks. Then Leo had a birthday. His parents gave him a BB gun. With Leo's past history, that was a very foolish gift. One afternoon I was invited down to his place to play. (We Nelson and Thompson kids usually played together twice a week.) As I looked over Leo's new acquisition I told him, "My folks don't believe in kids having guns."

"Girls not having guns, you mean. Men have to have guns to shoot coyotes and rabbits, Midge Thompson, and you know it. Besides, you ought to learn to shoot a gun too, if you're going to be a missionary. In Africa they've got rampagin' elephants and man-eatin' lions and—well, whatcha' gonna do without a gun? Tell me that, will ya?"

Leo's question made a circuit through my brain and made a connection. "Well, ah, maybe, just maybe, I'll have to learn to shoot a gun. If I go to Africa, that is."

"All right. Then let's get busy. I'll give you your first lesson now." Leo picked up his BB gun and looked for a target at which to aim. He spied his Mom's brand new, galvanized chicken water pan sitting on the back porch. It was about eighteen inches in diameter with a rim about five inches high. He decided that would make an excellent target. So he got some crayons and I colored a red, lopsided bull's-eye in the middle of the pan. I surrounded that with a two-inch, squiggly yellow band, and completed it with a two-inch blue band outside the yellow.

Then Leo nailed the pan to the tree and marked off a reasonable distance from which to shoot. He lifted the gun, leveled it at the target, closed one eye, and shot. He looked so professional as he pulled the trigger that I could hardly believe he hadn't landed a shot anywhere near the pan. His wide miss struck my funny bone, and I laughed up a storm. Leo didn't see any humor in that at all. Disgustedly, he handed me the gun. "Here, Miss Smarty! Ya' think it's so easy. Let's see ya' try it. I'll bet you'll hit something behind ya'."

I felt trapped into shooting the gun. I really had no desire to handle a gun at all, but now that I had made such a big deal out of Leo's failure, I felt I owed him the chance to ridicule me.

I picked up the gun, aimed it away from me, and pulled the trigger. Zing went the BB, landing right in the middle of the bull's-eye, penetrating the chicken pan. "Wow!" Leo exclaimed. "How did ya' do that? Ya' sure are a good shot. We ought to call ya' Annie Oakley."

I shrugged my shoulders since I was still numb from the shock of hitting anything. Besides, I wasn't about to admit that it was sheer luck rather than skill that I had hit the bull's-eye. I went over to the pan to examine the hole. Sure enough! I had made a perfect hit.

That was a challenge to Leo. He used up several boxes of BBs to prove that he could at least hit the pan. The poor chicken pan was so riddled with holes that it now resembled a sieve.

About then Annie came out on the veranda with a plate full of her spritz cookies. "Want some treats?" she asked pleasantly. My mouth watered as I looked at the goodies. But before she passed out the snack, her eyes followed the path from us to where we had been shooting. When she discovered her new chicken pan nailed to the tree and peppered with BB holes, she exploded. She called us some very irregular names and threatened to break the gun on us. I had never seen Annie so livid; I feared that my Mom would soon be bereft of a child. Leo tried to explain to her we hadn't planned that the BBs would go through the pan.

"Well, of all the stupid..." and Annie spent the next five minutes discrediting our intelligence. After Annie had denounced us sufficiently to release some of her stress, she told me to "GET RIGHT HOME." I revved up my muscles and took flight. I felt badly that I had made a hole in Annie's chicken pan, thus encouraging Leo to make more. I felt worse that I hadn't even had one spritz cookie. I was thankful, however, that she hadn't broken the gun on us.

As I walked into my kitchen door, I wasn't my buoyant self. Mom asked me why I had come home so early without Lela and Gladys. I told her that Annie was in a foul mood, and I was scared to be around her. Then she grilled me like a prosecuting attorney. It wasn't hard to get the truth from me. I was like an old refrigerator; I couldn't keep anything.

Mom sighed heavily. "You sure aren't learning very fast, are you? You still DO first and THINK later. That really was a dumb thing to do. How could you shoot at a pan and not make holes?" Then she said that Leo and I should pay for Annie's chicken pan. Mom had a Bible verse to back her up. My folks always did. "Exodus 22 means that if you destroy someone's property, you must make restitution, whether you did it willfully or accidentally," she explained. It meant that I would have to give much of my meager savings to Annie to pay for her chicken pan.

Before parting with my money, I told Mom that Leo was the one who had suggested our using the pan and had made all of the holes but one. But she wouldn't listen to any excuses. "If I have told you once, I have told you a hundred times, don't ever blame someone else if you yield to temptation. Remember? There is one word in the English language which ends all discussions. That word is…?"

Mom waited for me to fill in the blank. "No," I answered meekly.

"When you sin, it is you, and you alone, who could have prevented it. Don't ever blame anyone else. Your angel records your sins in your book, not Leo's. There is no excuse for sin, but there is forgiveness. When you steal from someone you must repay."

"But I didn't steal from Annie—just wrecked her pan. And only one of those holes was…" Mom didn't let me finish my sentence.

"You may as well have stolen the pan. She didn't have a pan to use when you kids finished with it, did she?"

I shook my head.

"All right, then. Take the responsibility for your actions. Damaging anyone's property is wrong. A 9-year-old girl should know that." Mom had just taught me another fundamental truth that surely is embedded somewhere in God's law of liberty. She had laid some pretty heavy stuff on me, but the principles she presented became a part of my moral fiber—if I damage anyone's property, I must make restitution.

In summers, Lela, Gladys, and I often practiced our aerial, trapeze, and rope walking routines in the new barn's haymow. A high platform on one end and a lower one on the other end with soft hay in the middle made this a relatively safe activity. (At least we thought so. Our parents hadn't voiced their opinion on the subject since they didn't know about this game). We were always trying to improve our techniques and to outdo one another. Since I was more than three years younger than Gladys and six and a half years younger than Lela, I always felt outdone by them. My most valiant attempts seemed amateurish— even to me.

Onc day we were practicing doing double somersaults as we leaped from the high platform down onto a pitifully small pile of hay. It was a dangerous thing to do because, if we missed the hay, we would fall at least 20 feet onto the wooden floor. Since it was that time of the summer when we had about run out of hay, Dad warned us not to play in the hay loft until he put in more hay. (He never knew what we were actually doing in the hay loft, or he'd have had heart failure. He probably thought we were just playing hide-and-seek).

By this time, we had become quite proficient in our aerial acts, so we chose to ignore his advice. Lela and Gladys began by making spectacular leaps, completing perfect double somersaults. Then I stretched my short legs to climb the long ladder leading to the high platform.

125

I almost grew dizzy as I looked at the great distance between me and the small heap of hay. But I screwed up my courage, leaped, spun, and completed a double somersault. I was drunk with success. I followed my sisters as we each turned another flawless performance. The third time I reached the platform, I was giddy with overconfidence, and I boasted, "Watch me! I'm going to do three somersaults!"

Before anyone could stop me, I gave a mighty leap, flew out too far, turned two and a half rounds, and landed on my head at the edge of the hay pile. As I slid rapidly down the pile, I raised my head to protect it, but I snapped my neck as I hit the floor. It knocked the wind out of me and a stabbing pain slithered down my spine. When I came to, Lela hovered over me, "Midge, are you hurt?"

Was I hurt!?!? My body couldn't help my mind discover the problem. It sent mixed messages to my brain— numbness, searing pain, nausea, dizziness, and a myriad of other nondescript feelings. I couldn't tell Lela what I felt since my brain couldn't sort things out.

Gladys got impatient, "Midge, are you going to die?" "I don't know," I moaned. "Probably. I think my neck is broken."

"Oh, no," Lela groaned. "Now what are we going to tell Dad? Midge, you can't die, you hear? I'll tell you what I'll do. I will pull your neck back into place if you'll promise not to tell."

I wasn't responsible for any statements I might have made in my semi-conscious state, but evidently Lela felt she had extracted my "last will and testament" approval from me. The next thing I knew Lela was yanking on my head while Gladys held my feet. There was excruciating pain, then my neck snapped, and the numbness gradually left my limbs. We will never know what was wrong with my neck, nor if my sisters performed a medical marvel. I do know that it hurt for me to turn my head or neck during the next month. Mom asked me repeatedly why I held my head so stiff. I told her I was "just training my neck to be straight." She shook her head. "Midge! Always full of crazy ideas!"

In my adult years doctors have puzzled over x-rays of my spine—especially the peculiar bone structure of my neck. They have suggested a break with calcification, arthritis, etc. I will forever bear the results of my disobedience in the hump in my neck. It remains as an object lesson to me: Though God forgives our sins, we still may carry the scars of them emotionally, mentally, or physically until we reach heaven.

Every summer Mom devoted unlimited time to her huge vegetable garden. Right after breakfast she marched off with her hoe to the garden, leaving us three girls to clear the table, wash the cream separator, make the beds, and clean the house. After we finished our chores, we were to join her in the garden.

Washing the separator was a detestable job, but Gladys was a good sport and almost always performed that task. Lela did other jobs while she kept up a constant chatter. She could be entertaining, but she could also be a pest. She didn't know when to stop her teasing before she made her victim angry. One day, as Gladys was washing the separator, Lela stood in the doorway of the pantry taunting her. "Are you about finished, GLAD ASS?"

"Shut up," Gladys retaliated. "And call me by my right name."

"I am, Miss GLAD ASS A DONKEY," answered Miss Smarty. "Why do you call her a donkey?" I asked innocently.

"Can't you figure it out? She is a GLAD ASS. Ass means donkey." Lela's eyes twinkled mischievously as she moved closer to Gladys.

Like a tornado, Gladys turned on Lela and gave her a mighty shove. Lela flew backwards, bounced off the wall, and landed in a very large farm pail half filled with milk. The milk made a sloshing, sucking sound and splattered all around her. Lela made a funny spectacle. She was doubled up with her bottom stuck in the pail, flailing her arms and legs. I thought I had never seen anything so funny and laughed hysterically.

"So you think that's funny?" Gladys said, glaring at me. "You'd best not tell Mom, or you'll be in for it." I never bothered to find out what I would be in for because Gladys was advancing menacingly in my direction. I knew that we kids almost never hit one another, but this time the gleam in Gladys' eyes seemed to indicate otherwise. I fled from her presence as Jacob did from Esau, and ran to the garden where Mom was working.

"What do you want, Midge?" Mom asked suspiciously.

"Oh, nothing," I lied. I really wanted protection from her other kid but didn't dare say so. I was small, while Gladys had grown into a tall, strong girl. Comparing our physiques and Gladys' mood, I believed I was wise to run.

"Have you finished your chores?" Mom questioned. "I've done as much as I can. So I, ah, thought I'd weed my beets."

"That's a good idea," Mom agreed, seeming satisfied with my explanation. "Why don't you do your row, then finish mine. I'll go to the carrots. They're harder to weed."

I readily agreed to her plan. Trading a little extra work for Mom's protection seemed like a good deal at the moment. And you can bet, I never told Mom of that morning's episode. That summer, I learned that I could keep a secret if it was a matter of life or death.

Autumn

Autumn brought an end to our long, happy summers. We returned to school with a degree of enthusiasm because it was fun being back with the community kids again and playing together at recesses.

Autumn frosts brought down colored leaves for us to pile up and jump into. There were carrots and beets to dig and store in piles of sand in the cellar, and potatoes to pick from our field and store in another bin. We viewed with pride the hundreds of quarts of fruits and vegetables we had preserved for winter's use sitting on the basement shelves. We helped Dad pull the last loads of hay into the haymow and pick the ripe corn. We watched the ducks and Canada geese fly south for the winter. We carved pumpkins for decoration. After dusk, we caught the young chickens roosting in the evergreens and put them into the chicken house for protection against the cold and the animal predators. Then we came in from the cold to savor Mom's fresh doughnuts and hot chocolate.

One autumn night I was sleeping downstairs in Grandmother's bedroom when I heard Fido making a big fuss in the front yard. I glanced out the window, and my heart nearly stopped. I saw two men carrying gunny sacks and keeping Fido at bay by poking him with long sticks. I knew they were thieves going after the chickens roosting in the evergreens. I wanted to stop them because it meant money to us—we were going to sell them in a few days. At first I was too scared to move, but when I heard the chickens squawking as the thieves grabbed them from the trees and stuffed them into their sacks, I moved into action. I crawled on my hands and knees to the stairs; then I ran up the steps and called Nels. He jumped out of bed, raced down the stairs, grabbed the double barrel shot gun, and ran to the door. "Get out of there, you crooks," Nels yelled and then pulled the trigger. He purposely shot over their heads, but it made the thieves know he meant business. They dropped their sacks and ran. Fido raced after them, snatched away a few souvenirs from their pants, and came home with his trophies. I never, ever, forgot that night.

Autumn was not my favorite season. It reminded me of death—everything withered and died. I said good-bye to the birds, the morning glories, and my favorite apple tree. Yet I knew they would be resurrected in the spring, just like people will when Jesus returns. The thought filled my childish heart with love for God and anticipation for the spring of life when God will make all things new.

Chapter 15

Making Machines and Money

It had been over a year since my bout with mastoid and rheumatic fever, but I still suffered with pain in my joints at night. During the daytime, I had learned to ignore the pain. And when Leo arrived on the scene, we found enough exciting things to do that diverted our attention from anything mundane.

One day as we wandered through our grove of trees trying to settle on a plan for the day, Leo stopped suddenly, his eyes resting on the wheels and chassis of an old buggy. He studied the contraption, walking around it, looking under it, and acting like a genius at work. From the intense look on his face I knew that Leo was hatching up some super brilliant scheme. I waited breathlessly for him to divulge his inspiration. "Midge," he began slowly with an air of importance. Then a long, suspenseful pause ensued.

"What? WHAT?" I shouted anxiously, unable to contain myself longer.

"We will invent a new mode of transportation from this buggy. Let the other kids ride horses and bikes. We'll ride in an automo-buggy."

My elation over Leo's plan couldn't be measured. He had my complete support. I threw my arms around him, but he pushed me away before I could kiss him. "Don't get mushy. After all, we are old now—nine and ten."

I'll never know why it never dawned on us that Henry Ford had already perfected his horseless carriage about 20 years earlier. Model A touring cars stood in both of our garages. But, I suppose, our dream vehicle was so primitive in comparison to Henry Ford's black, shiny inventions that we never made the connection. Besides, this would give us our own mode of transportation.

Dad, with an indulgent grin, gave us permission to use the old buggy and his workshop. For the few days we worked on our invention. Leo did the mechanics; I handed him the tools. He was lucky that I knew that much. He attached his mother's Maytag washing machine motor to a board we fastened to the middle of the buggy frame. Next Leo hitched a pulley from the motor to the back wheel of the buggy. Leo did some other improvisations that I didn't understand nor could I explain. Steering the machine would be no problem. We used the same method our sisters had used a few years earlier. We tied a rope to both ends of the front axle; thus we could maneuver the vehicle by pulling on the rope in the direction we wished to turn. Our sisters had pushed the buggy; we would ride.

The day came for our trial run. Of course, our sisters were on hand to ridicule our "crude contraption," but they could not squelch our enthusiasm. Our Buggymobile, as we called it, ran real well on level ground, but when we came to any kind of incline, it just sputtered. Since Leo had determined that he, and he alone, would drive it, that left me riding the back board. Whenever the machine halted, Leo would yell, "Midge, jump off and push."

"Why me?" I asked, objecting to the job relegated to me. "Why do I have to do all the pushing? I'm tired and sweating, and I've pushed for two days. I want to drive."

"You can't drive. You're a girl, and everyone knows that girls can't drive," Leo said with finality. I kept quiet but was seething inside. Once more I asked God to make me a boy and to please hurry up about it.

Leo and I were the envy of the neighborhood kids, even if our sisters thought nothing of our triumph. The attention we got from the other kids made us feel famous. We privately hoped that Henry Ford would get wind of our inventive genius and ask us to go into partnership with him. (Actually, Leo was the genius; I barely knew enough to be the tool handler). But before we could patent our invention, Annie, Leo's mother, ruined everything. She demanded her washing machine motor be returned immediately. Then she threatened, "And don't let me catch you Katzenjammer Kids touching my washing machine motor again! Ever!" She said considerable more, but it probably should not be recorded here. In any case, we were duly impressed. When Annie talked that loud and that tough, we listened. Since Annie had confiscated her engine and my Dad offered us none of his, we were forced to turn our interest from inventing to making money.

In those days, South Dakota grain fields were being overrun by gophers. Those pesky critters added further to their unpopularity by digging holes in the pastures; when farm animals stepped into these holes, they could break a leg. So the government offered a bounty of five cents per gopher tail that was sent to the county office. Leo and I figured we'd cash in on this bonanza. It seemed like an honest way of getting rich and helping the community at the same time. So we set traps, snagged five gophers and sent the tails to the courthouse in Flandreau.

We were thrilled when we received our first quarter by return mail. But how do you divide a quarter? Leohad the solution. He would take 13 cents, and I'd have to settle for the 12 cents. I knew I would continue to get gypped; so the next time I insisted that we send in ten tails, netting us each a quarter. Annie and Mom agreed that we should take turns sharing the three-cent postage cost too. So during the summer of my fourth grade year, we were having a wonderful and profitable time. I suspect that our parents were thankful that our interest had been channeled into a respectable activity.

One Saturday night when we were in town, I overheard Mom and Annie talking with some neighbor ladies on the bench outside of Barnes Store. Someone must have asked what their Katzenjammer Kids were up to this summer, because Annie answered defensively, a hint of steel in her voice. "They are doing great. Actually, those two are using their energies profitably—each has earned over a dollar this summer catching gophers. And they're cutting down on the gopher population. We can already tell the difference in our crops and garden with less gophers. What are your kids doing?"

I could tell by the way Annie talked that it was one thing for her to call us Katzenjammer Kids when she was mad at us; it was quite another thing for the neighbors to do so. I hoped that Annie's testimonial would set things straight, and that the neighbors would stop thinking of us as mischievous, comic-strip characters. We wished to be known as useful citizens. Ah, yes! WE WOULD SHOW THEM!

With renewed vigor we expanded our trapping territory. People were quite willing for us to trap on their land, but we got tired of walking a mile for a gopher. When school started, we noticed that there were a lot of gophers on the prairie across from the school. This virgin territory needed our help badly, but all of our traps were in use. Leo suggested that we drown out the gophers and kill them with a ball bat as they escaped their burrows. This seemed like a more humane way to kill them anyway— swiftly and painlessly. We really liked the little creatures, but the excess of gophers had narrowed the contest down to them or the farmers. Men trappers had killed off the foxes and coyotes, their natural enemies, thus causing a gopher explosion.

Leo and I began drowning out the gophers across from the school. It was a success from the start. As usual, Leo took charge of these operations. He sent me to fill two pails with water from the school's well, while he kept watch on a hole that we had just seen a gopher enter. I lugged the heavy buckets, slopping water in my shoes. Then I poured the water down the holes, while King Leo stood ready with his ball bat. Leo was an accurate whacker, and the gopher died immediately. Reason told me that we were doing a useful, necessary thing, but my emotions were at variance with my common sense. I discussed with Leo my desire to cease gopher operations before the following great hurrah took place.

One day after school, when the other kids had gone home, Leo and I crossed the road from the school to the prairie. "It looks like we've killed all the gophers in the holes nearest the school," he commented.

"Yep! And it's too far for me to carry water anymore. I resign."

"Not so fast. Let's try the easiest method. Go back of the school barn and get the paper sack full of stuff that I left there this morning. Meanwhile I'll find a lived-in gopher hole."

I might have known that I'd be the "go-for" person, but I acquiesced and shortly returned with his bag. In it he had a box of matches, a small bottle of kerosene, and some rags. Besides the bat that he carried, he also had a short stick. He tied the rags to the stick, soaked them in kerosene, and told me, "No more carrying water! From now on, we're going to smoke out the gophers!"

I gasped. "Do you really think we should? We aren't supposed to play with matches."

"Who's playing?" he questioned incredulously. "We're working hard to rid this community of the gopher plague. The farmers are too busy to do this, and the women won't. Don't you know that if the American farmer doesn't grow grain, the rest of the world will starve? You claim you're going to be a missionary! Huh! This is your mission work now!" Leo sniffed and sighed, leaving me to feel that I had abandoned my mission in life before I had even begun.

I shrugged my shoulders. I couldn't think of a good answer right then. So when Leo handed me the match box, I lit the rags. Leo pushed the torch down into a hole and soon the gopher came rushing out of his emergency exit not the one where Leo held the torch. Leo threw down the torch, picked up his bat and started chasing the victim. But the gopher had a head start and slipped through the tall grass easily. Leo, on the other hand, got tangled in the grass and kept falling as he raced after the gopher. The gopher led Leo in a wild chase before he ducked into another burrow. All the while I enjoyed the hilarious scene and indulged in some thigh-slapping guffaws. Leo returned to where I was, still doubled up with laughter. He was sullen and angry, so I reined in my laughter immediately. Silently we faced each other, trying to regain our composure. Then we were startled into a panic. We first smelled the smoke of the dried prairie grass burning; then we looked to where Leo had thrown the burning fagot and I had thrown the match. A strong west wind was whipping the two fires toward us. We knew we needed to move out of the pathway the blaze was taking. So we ran north along the edge of the fire and then west to the road. Just then a car came along. We stopped him and told him to go to the first farmhouse (mine) and tell them that the prairie was on fire. The man sped off almost before we finished talking.

Evidently the man delivered the message, and Mom made a general ring on the party line because soon men began to arrive from all over. Dad pulled a flatbed with barrels of water to the fire's edge, and men with soaked gunnysacks beat at the flames. Before the fire reached our cornfield on the south and Scrivens on the east, the men had the fire out.

All the while I had been praying that God would help the men stop the fire. I knew that our carelessness might result in great loss of crops and even our farm buildings. The men, covered with soot and sweat, gathered by the side of the road to recap their heroic efforts. Leo and I mingled among them. Some men even commended us for reporting the fire. My conscience could hardly stand this praise because they didn't know we had started the fire in the first place. We had done well to stop the car, but if it had not been for the quick response of the neighborhood men there is no telling what a calamity might have occurred that day.

The men decided that the fire had been started by a cigarette flipped from a passing car. This may have been true because there was a big burned area by the road that connected with our torch area. The wind was from the west that day, and it is impossible for a fire to burn against the wind. Nonetheless, what someone else's carelessness might have done did not relieve me of my sense of guilt. We too, had started a fire. Leo, however, persuaded me not to tell what we had perpetrated. He said it would disgrace our parents in the eyes of the neighbors, and there was nothing we could do to change what had been done

Something good came out of that fire, however. It killed much of the gopher population, and it burned the bad weeds. At the same time, it left the roots of the good grass. "Nothing like a good cleansing fire," Dad commented. "Only I wouldn't have picked such a windy day to do it." But even Dad's remark did not soothe my guilty conscience. Did he suspect something?

The next spring the grass came up more beautiful than ever. Sort of the way the new earth will appear after God cleanses the old with fire, I thought.

My zeal for earning money had waned. Winter came and covered the ground with snow. Our trapping days were over.

Chapter 16

A Visit From Real Live Missionaries

"Carl, Alice, and the children are coming home on furlough this summer and will spend several weeks with us," Mrs. Flatten announced one Sabbath in church. This most exciting news sent me into orbit. I was going to get to see some real, live missionaries and the lady for whom I had been named (Alice Flatten Christensen). You couldn't beat that for thrills! From my earliest recollections I had drunk in the stories of missions and missionaries. Once in awhile we'd get to see them at camp meeting, but to have some right in our own church, have them home for meals, and talk with them face to face! That was the closest thing to walking and talking with angels, I believed. So I practiced being good. I wanted to make a good impression. If righteousness by works counted for anything, I surely deserved a set of wings and a halo. But all I got was questions from my family—"Midge, are you feeling okay?"

I did everything that was asked of me and even volunteered for other jobs. Fortunately for me, no one pressed their luck, and I was able to maintain sainthood for the next few weeks.

The day finally came when I got to meet Alice Flatten. I was awed in her presence. "So this is Alice Mildred," she said gathering me into her arms. "You are blond just like

I am, but you have curly hair. Would you share some with your namesake?"

Would I!?! I would have given her my best doll and thrown in my cousin Leo to boot!! But at that point I couldn't get either my tongue or voice to function. Alice assured me that she was just joking and then introduced me to her children—Charles, Marjorie, and Marilyn. I studied the family carefully. They looked so ah, so ordinary. Yes, very HUMAN. I had thought that missionaries would have a distinctive aura about them—like a cross between a human and an angel, maybe.

Despite their regular-people appearance, I found the Christensen family to be very special. They exuded gracious, loving Christianity—even the children. They may not have looked like angels, but I thought their demeanor was within the celestial range. I managed to capture a front-row seat and listened enraptured to Carl and Alice relate their mission experiences. They wore costumes from South America and showed us memorabilia they had collected. I clung to their words and could repeat every story they told. As far as I was concerned, they were the most important people that ever landed in Colman. And, I was equally positive the best profession in the world was to be a missionary ON FURLOUGH. I imagined how wonderful it would be to keep people spellbound with mission stories; I wasn't certain, however, that I wanted to experience six years of hardship and dangers out there on the front line first. But my sisters insisted that real missionaries took the tough part before they enjoyed the furlough bonus.

For the next few weeks my every waking moment focused on the Christensen family. Leo felt neglected and thought I was becoming a zealot; but I didn't care what Leo said because the missionaries' visit helped me zero in on my life plans. I decided that I would become a teacher and ask God to give me a mission field. From the Christensens I understood more clearly why foreign mission work was so important. Missionaries literally fulfill Jesus' commission to go into all the world and preach the gospel. Because God loved us so much that He came down to this earth to die for our sins. We, in gratitude, need to take His message of love to the world so His Kingdom will be filled with grateful, happy souls. Carl said it wouldn't be fair for us to keep the gospel of salvation just for Americans. God could use angels, but He gives humans the privilege of being His ambassadors. There is no higher calling than that. Therefore, missionaries go forward in faith, willing to live or die to deliver this good news.

When I grasped this concept, it was no longer vital to me to be a missionary on furlough. I was willing to be a regular missionary and endure "the tough part." And if I lived until furlough time, that would be God's extra bonus to me. I could not have defended the fine points of Biblical doctrine at that time, but my determination to serve God could not have been more sincere. From that time I had the distinct impression that I would someday be called to work in a mission field. There would be times when that vision would be blurred and almost fade into oblivion, but my childhood covenant with God is my life today.

I was sorry to see the Christensen family return to South America. When Alice kissed me good-bye, I shared my decision with her. "Some-day I'm going to be a missionary too."

Alice hugged me again. "I'm sure you will. God will help you keep that promise." Of course, she spoke encouragingly to me. She had grown up in the Colman Church, and it was her nature.

Another summer we had ex-missionaries from India come to the farm. The Alfred Youngberg family was now on permanent return to the states, but their visit was nonetheless exciting to me. My parents were always happy to see the Youngbergs. Alfred, his brother Gus, and sister Ruth had been baptized into our fledgling Colman church in 1913. Subsequently, all three Youngbergs had become missionaries, and it was with pride that the Colman people welcomed them home.

All of this happened a decade before I was born, so I had never seen the Youngbergs. But the fact that they had been missionaries certainly threw me into a tizzy of excitement. Even the knowledge that they had already been back from India for four years didn't minimize my expectations.

My cup of joy spilled over when the Youngbergs arrived with their six children. The kids ranged in age from baby John to 12-year-old Steven. They would stay a whole week with us while Mother helped Mrs. Youngberg with her sewing. Mom was an artistic wonder when it came to sewing. She only needed to look at the dress style we chose from the Montgomery Ward catalog, and she could reproduce it exactly. She began by cutting a pattern for herself out of newspapers, holding it against us for size, making adjustments, and then cutting it out of the material. Before nightfall, the dress would be finished and pressed. Sometimes we girls complicated her sewing by selecting a neck line from one dress, a bodice from another, and a skirt from still another. This never stymied Mom. That same day we would have a stylish dress not even found in the catalog. No wonder Mrs. Youngberg had come to Mom to help her outfit Margaret and Olive for the summer.

While Mom was busy with Mrs. Youngberg, Lela was given charge of the household chores. She and Gladys invented a dozen ingenious ways of getting the Youngberg kids and me involved in the work. We were happy to cooperate because when the work was done my sisters played hide-and-seek with us, helped us walk on stilts or on rolling barrels, and did other fun things. But the most fun we had was polishing the dining room floor. After Lela washed the dining room floor, she put on a thick layer of paste wax. When it dried, she gave each of us kids an old pair of Dad's woolen socks to wear. Then she led us in a glorious chase, slipping and sliding all over the floor. "Slide clear to the edge of the wall and rub your feet about," Lela instructed. We kids had two hours of marvelous fun, and wise Lela got her floor polished to a mirror-like reflection.

The Youngberg children were well behaved. Following their example, I would have taken another journey into sainthood had it not been for Russell. Although he was a couple of years younger, he was as big as I was so I considered him an equal. His undaunted devotion to my lead enticed me to trespass my father's rules like swimming in the horse tank and riding the calves, an activity strictly forbidden by Dad since our weight could injure the backbones of the growing animals. When I swung high from the ropes in the haymow, Russell was flush with admiration, "Wow! I'll bet not even the monkeys in India can do that!" I took that as the best of compliments and

143

thought the young man had astute judgment. I coveted Russell's adulation so I hung from my heels high up on the windmill crossbars and performed other dangerous feats to impress him. Russell probably thought I was the world's biggest show-off, and he would have been right. But he was too nice to say anything unkind.

I did have my nicer moments too. Margaret was my age and a lovely girl. She was so careful with my dolls and other toys that I knew I could trust her with my favorite things. There was only one thing about Margaret that I didn't like—the way she was dressed. She wore dresses that were about three inches below her knees and black stockings. Knee-length dresses and anklets were in vogue for girls our age, so I was ashamed to be seen with Margaret in public.

One day Mom decided to take Mrs. Youngberg into Colman to shop for dress material. She loaded a 24-dozen crate of eggs into the trunk of the car to pay for the material. Then Lela drove Mrs. Youngberg, Russell, Margaret, Olive, Mom, and I into town. While the ladies used up the egg money selecting dress materials, Mother sent me over to the drug store to buy ice cream cones for the Youngberg children and myself. I didn't mind being seen with the boys. They were dressed in the shirts and overalls that Dad bought them, so they looked like the farm boys of our community. But Margaret and Olive were garbed in those long dresses! I was embarrassed and hoped that none of my friends would chance to see us. I hurried them in and out of the drugstore and back to where Mom was still figuring yardage. But my Mother was a discerning soul, and when she noticed that I had separated myself from Margaret, she detected my character flaw. When we got home, Mom talked to me. She quickly identified my problem as PRIDE, the sin that caused Lucifer to be cast out of heaven. She elaborated on that for a spell and then proceeded with a sermonette that has stuck with me for life.

"Midge, do you think you are better in the eyes of God than Margaret?"

"But she looks funny in those long dresses and black stockings," I protested.

"I see. Midge looks on the outward appearance, but God looks on your and Margaret's hearts," she paraphrased. "What do you think God is seeing in your heart? He sees that Margaret's heart is quite pure—free from pride, full of kindness..." and she continued to list Margaret's many virtues. I got the point, felt ashamed of my attitude, and was ready to leave. But Mother wasn't finished.

"Do you realize, Midge, that you are really no better dressed than anyone else? With the exception of the three new cotton dresses I make you girls each summer, all of your clothes are handed down from your sisters, which come secondhand to them from friends or your cousins in Iowa. So what you wear is third-time-arounders. I always try to redo them in some way to make you feel they are new or different."

Come to think of it, that was true. All of my winter clothes were remakes. The only new coat I ever had (until I got to college) was the blue-plaid blazer my sister Jennie gave me the first year she taught school. But Mom fixed my clothes up so nicely that no one seemed to notice my third-hand garb. I was aware that the other girls at church and school often had store-bought clothes, but that did not concern me since I was satisfied with mine.

Before I got the clothes situation into proper perspective, Mom continued, "Now, Midge, people a have a right to wear what they feel is comfortable and right in God's eyes. Modesty is a fine virtue, and the Youngberg girls are dressed modestly. They are clean and neat children. They are well-behaved and devoted little Christians. Now, if God sees Margaret and Olive as children fit for His house, are they not good enough for yours? If they are His special friends, aren't they good enough to be yours?"

WOW! Mom had hit me with a double whammy. But there was more. "The Youngberg children are every bit as intelligent as you are, and one day they will make great contributions to the world, and God will be so proud of them. Will you do more because you wear shorter dresses and anklets? Will you make God proud of you? Looks, intelligence, talents—all these are gifts from God. We do nothing to deserve these blessings. As God gives, He may also take away. Some people use God's gifts to benefit themselves, while others use the gifts to bless others. The two talents everyone can use are kindness and humility. You will be happier if you use them both. Can I count on you?"

Mother left me a legacy that day. I have never forgotten those pearls of truth. And I am a happier person because I know that anything I am able to accomplish in life, even any goodness in me, is a gift from God. Since then, I have tried to treat people as Jesus would treat them.

With my prejudices gone, I spent the next few days having a wonderful time with Margaret. She was not only beautiful outwardly, but radiantly beautiful within. I longed to be just like her and was sorry to see her leave.

The next time I met the Youngbergs was at the South Dakota camp meeting held on the state fairgrounds at Huron. Housing for the campers was provided in the exhibition buildings where separate rooms were partitioned off with canvass. Smaller buildings were used for the children, youth, adult, and German meetings and a camp store. My family always enjoyed this spiritual retreat and the reprieve from the farm work. We three girls and Mom were slightly scrunched in our cubicle—four cots, a table, two chairs, a cupboard made by putting one apple box on top of another to store food, and a corner for hanging our clothes. But I loved this primitive camping; it stirred my pioneer spirit.

One day after the children's meeting, I met Russell. He remembered my proclivity for excitement so suggested that he and I skip the afternoon children's meeting and go investigate the grandstand and arena area which were basically closed for our usage. Russell's idea sounded scintillating to me, so when Mom left for her afternoon meeting, I walked towards mine—my meeting with Russell. Perhaps Russell had gotten permission to skip the children's meeting, but I had not; so while he had a clear conscience, I did not. But as soon as we crawled through a hole in the fence into the arena, my conscience was diverted from its proper function by the grandeur of the place. Russell challenged me to race him to the top of the grandstand. Though he was younger than I, he was big and strong, so we were about equal competitors. We had a great time leaping from one row of bleachers to the next, up and down, down and up. At last we wearied of our sport. Since it was about time for the meetings to be over, I figured I had better get back to the room and clean up.

But it was a futile task. My shoes were muddy, my dress dirty from the dusty bleachers, my curls tangled, and my ribbons askew. I also had some purple bumps and bloody scratches on my shins from missing the bleachers.

I had scarcely begun the cleaning process when Mom walked into the room and scrutinized me. Her brows furrowed. "Just where have you been, young lady?" she asked, obviously upset.

I wasn't good at making up stories. Further, anyone with an ounce of reason would know that I hadn't accumulated that amount of damage at a children's meeting. So I just blurted out the truth and left the rest to the mercy of my mother. I hoped that the camp meeting spirit had taken enough control of her so that she would resist inflicting physical pain upon me.

"What shall I do with you?" she asked sitting down and looking at the floor. She sounded tired and disappointed. I loved her so much I was suddenly very sorry that I had caused her this pain. I couldn't resist the impulse —I ran over and threw my arms around her and hugged her. I told her how sorry I was and that I would accept, without resentment, any punishment she felt I deserved. I already had received the worst punishment—the disappointed look on her face.

"Midge, you should have asked my permission before you ran off to do anything like that. There is a degree of trust that families must have in one another. If I go somewhere, I tell you. If you want to go somewhere, you should ask me."

"I know, Mom, but Russell..."

"Midge, are you going to try to excuse yourself and lay the blame on Russell? You know that never works with your papa and me. There is no excuse for yielding to temptation—ever! God gives each of us the power to resist it. There is one word in the English language that answers all temptations—NO! Don't blame anyone else for the things you do. Do you remember that verse in the Bible that says that even a child is known by his doings? I would think that after being called a Katzenjammer Kid for so long you would know that. God loves you and has paid for your sins, but you must do your part too. No one else can do that for you.

"Now, since the Christensens and the Youngbergs have been around, you have grown spiritually. I don't want you to feel discouraged because you slip backward once in awhile. But are you happy that you slipped this afternoon? Couldn't you have done that excursion between meetings when you were more appropriately dressed, with permission? What you did was deceptive. You wanted to make me think you were at the meeting when you were not. Do you think that sort of thing will be acceptable in life?"

Mom had given me a lot to think about, and I was contrite. I never wanted to disappoint her again. And I certainly wanted to feel a kinship with God. From that day on, I found it much easier to stand for principle and resist temptations. I learned to use that one word in the English language—NO.

Alfred Youngberg Family

Steven, Margaret, Russell, and Gordon became medical doctors.

Olive married a history professor.

John has his Ph.D. and teaches at Andrews University.

Carl Christensen Family

Charles, Marjorie and Marilyn all got college degrees and worked for the church.

Chapter 17

The
Little White Church
on the Hill

When I was only two weeks old my parents bundled me up and tucked me under the buffalo robe in the horse-drawn sled for the 25-minute dash over crunching snow to our small country church. That sacred spot became the center of my spiritual life. There I first sensed the holy presence of God; there I learned to reverence, worship, and love Him in a special way.

In this little white church on the hill my home religious training was enhanced and augmented by my church family. They didn't just talk about love, they shared it; they didn't just talk about faith, they practiced it; they didn't just talk about sacrifice, they did it. The adults in my church were fathers and mothers and older brothers and sisters to all of us children. They specialized in caring about kids. They shared their time, advice, and encouragement with us, the same as with their peers. They built our self-esteem by giving us simple church responsibilities, and then making sure we succeeded in our tasks. They deserved the compliments for our successes but made sure we got the praise. They made us know we were important to them and to God. This is why, as far as I know, our little church (with never a baptized membership of more than 34 persons) produced more church workers and missionaries per capita than probably any other church in the world.

Walking back through memory's lane, I see the pews where each family sat—the Flattens, Olsons, Otters, Priors, Scrivens, Simmermans, and Thompsons. (In my teens, the Ochengas, Warners, Kansanbacks, and Neptunes joined). In my reverie I hear once more a Thirteenth Sabbath program, the mission stories, the testimony meetings. And I cherish the principles our church founders helped instill into us.

Our little church had a humble beginning, which was nonetheless miraculous. Shortly after the marriage of my parents on November 30, 1904, God impressed my father to improve his English by comparing the Danish and English Bibles. Of course, he started with Genesis and the creation story. In the second chapter, he confronted an idea foreign to his Danish Lutheran upbringing. He realized, for the first time, that God had added a seventh-day at the end of His work week. That seventh-day was God's special gift to man—a day for rest and sacred worship.

Dad turned to his Lutheran pastor, thrilled with his discovery. He trusted that a man of the cloth would be happy to learn that the seventh-day was the true Sabbath and honest enough to rectify the church's error. Not so.

"No, Martin," the pastor contended. "Jesus changed the day from Sabbath to Sunday when he was crucified. We keep Sunday in honor of Jesus' resurrection."

"But Jesus never told us to do that," Dad disputed, disappointed with the pastor's response. "He even rested in the tomb on the Sabbath, not resuming His work until Sunday morning. After I read Genesis 2, I researched every text pertaining to the Sabbath. Jesus even said that he made the Sabbath for man, and not man for the Sabbath. Worshipping on the Sabbath was one of the very first things God asked man to do. God must have suspected that man might be tempted to appropriate the Sabbath hours for something else. That's why in the fourth commandment He told us to REMEMBER the Sabbath day to keep it holy. That's the day we are to worship Him, the creator of heaven and earth. Don't you see?"

"No, Martin, I don't see! And don't go quoting scripture to me. I am a graduate of the seminary and am learned in such matters. You have only an eighth grade education..."

"Fifth," Dad corrected. "And I do respect your training. But, please, just show me one Bible text that says we should keep Sunday. Greta would like that."

"Well, there isn't one. But keeping Saturday would identify us with the Jews, so Christians keep Sunday in honor of the resurrection."

"You said that before, and that's not a good reason if it's man's idea. God blessed, sanctified, and hallowed the seventh day, and man can't change what God ordained."

"Martin, you are a good man, but you'd better leave biblical interpretation to me and tend to your farm and your family. By the way, how are Greta, Nels, little Dorathy and your parents?" The minister asked, cunningly redirecting the conversation.

Dad knew that the conversation was over as far as the minister was concerned. He left the pastor's house, more disillusioned than ever with his Lutheran religion. But Dad continued to read his Bible, learning more new truths not taught by his church.

"Just listen to this, Greta," Dad urged, exuding the excitement he felt as he sat studying by the lamp light, ferreting out Biblical information. "I'm only in the second chapter of the Bible, and I've discovered another major discrepancy in the tenets of our Lutheran faith. It's about the state of the dead. According to scripture, the body plus the breath makes the soul. Therefore, when one dies, there is no soul or spirit to ascend into glory. When the breath is gone, the body goes to the grave to await the resurrection. Then when Jesus comes the second time in all His glory, He recreates the bodies of the righteous dead, gives them breath, and takes them to heaven along with the righteous living. Isn't that something?"

"I know what is SOMETHING—your getting all those crazy ideas from the Old Testament," Mom muttered, rocking Dorathy so vigorously that she awakened the child. Displeasure with Dad's religious zeal was reflected in her scowl, but Dad was too preoccupied to notice.

"Oh, well, Greta, the New Testament teaches the same thing. I've read every text that has anything to do with death and immortality, I think. The Bible has hundreds of them. They all teach the same thing. This one from the New Testament is very clear: Paul writes, "I would not have you ignorant, brethren, concerning them which are asleep, that you sorrow not, even as others which have no hope. For if we believe that Jesus died and rose again, even so them also which sleep in Jesus will God bring with Him.... We which are alive and remain unto the coming of the Lord shall not precede them which are asleep. For the Lord Himself shall descend from heaven with a shout, and the voice of the archangel, and with the trump of God. And the dead in Christ shall rise first; then we which are alive and remain shall be caught up together with them in the clouds, to meet the Lord in the air; so shall we ever be with the Lord.' That's I Thessalonians 4. 1 Corinthians 15 says..."

"Martin, I don't want to hear it. My mother, father, and sister died and went to heaven. I don't want to believe anything else. Just stop reading the Bible! You're a farmer, not a preacher. Besides, you are upsetting our minister and me with your 'Bible truths,' as you call them." With those remarks, Mom stomped off to the bedroom.

But no one could discourage Dad, who, by nature, was a scholar. He continued to read the Bible, and by using his little concordance and the marginal references he compared text with text.

In late May of 1908, Jack, a young colporteur, arrived at the Colman train station. He planned to sell Bible Readings for the Home Circle books in Moody County—called a dark county because there were no Adventists there. But now that Jack had reached his destination, his courage almost failed. He dreaded the challenge, worried that he would be rebuffed and fail. Storing his trunk at the train depot, Jack stepped outside and prayed silently for God to guide him to the right people. Then he picked up his briefcase and walked out of town, feeling impressed that the farmers might be more receptive to his work than the town folks. Jack walked past farm after farm, trying to muster courage to begin his task.

He finally found himself three and a half miles out of town, still procrastinating. He scolded himself for his cowardice. Suddenly he felt impressed to visit the next farmhouse. This was as God had planned it, but Jack didn't know it then.

Jack walked up our long lane and found Dad, his first customer, hitching up the bay team to the mower. Dad listened politely to Jack's canvass, even though he was somewhat skeptical of books that taught religion. "Just a minute, young man," Dad interrupted, "I'm willing to buy your book if, and only if, it teaches pure Bible truth. I won't accept man-made doctrine. Before I put money down on your book, please tell me what does it say about death?"

"Ah, it, ah, takes the texts right from the Bible," the colporteur hedged, not wanting to spoil his first sale in this Lutheran community.

"Oh, come now. Surely you can give me a more straightforward answer than that, if indeed you understand it yourself," Dad challenged impatiently. "I'm a busy man. This is the beginning of the haying season for the summer, so I don't have time to listen to a young upstart sidestep the issues."

Jack's face flushed as he shifted nervously from one foot to the other. Then, fearing that his colporteur career had ended already, he just blurted out, "Dead people are asleep and buried and know nothing until the resurrection at the second coming of Jesus."

"Good," Dad agreed, smiling. "Now we are getting somewhere. Does your book teach that heaven will be filled with immortal, flesh-and-blood people?"

The colporteur nodded, uncomfortably confounded by this farmer. He had lost control of the canvass—the customer was in charge. It wasn't supposed to happen this way. The literature evangelist leader never covered this lesson in salesmanship. Further, Jack had been told that this was a dark county. Now the first person he meets talks for all the world like a Seventh-day Adventist. Jack did not enjoy being grilled by Dad about the doctrine taught in his book, so he pressed for a sale. But Dad would have none of that evasiveness.

"There is still one more important difference between what I believe and what my church teaches. I've learned that the seventh-day, Saturday, is the true Sabbath. I have started to worship alone on that day. I still take Greta to church on Sundays. Greta, that's my wife, is from Germany. Her family was mistreated by some Jews and so she doesn't want anything to do with an idea that seems Jewish. What does your book say about the Sabbath?"

The colporteur knew very well what his book said about the Sabbath, but was too overwhelmed by the Biblical knowledge of this farmer to form a simple reply. So he slipped his Bible out from his brief case, and the two men sat down under the cottonwood tree in the farmyard to study the basic tenets of the Adventist faith. The horses, still hitched to the mower, swished the flies away with their silky tails as they stood sleepily waiting for the command of their master. But their master was so intensely involved in Bible study that he forgot his work.

By noon, Jack was convinced that he had found a fellow believer. "Do you know what?" he questioned enthusiastically. "You are a Seventh-day Adventist!"

"A what?" Dad asked, drawing back.

"You're a Seventh-day Adventist! You believe the doctrines taught by the Adventist church. How did you learn them? I was told there were no Adventists in this county."

Now it was Dad's turn to be confused. "Well, friend, I can assure you I am not a seven-day Advent. I never heard of such people. I just read the Bible and try to follow it. My minister says God's not that particular. What I can't understand is why God bothered to preserve the Bible, pure and complete, through all of these centuries if it's not important. The Bible and what it teaches is important to me. So I've lost interest in my church. I like the pastor, but his message seems shallow—like he's denying truth."

Their extended study was interrupted by Mom who called the two in for dinner. Hospitality was, and still is, a common practice in the Dakota farming community. Anyone on the premises at mealtime is invited to eat with the family.

Mom didn't mind having a dinner guest, but she minded very much that Dad had wasted the morning talking instead of mowing the hay. She told him so in German.

But Dad was too engrossed in the religious scene to notice her censure. In fact, he could hardly wait for the colporteur to finish the blessing to divulge his good news. "Greta, I just learned that I do belong to a church. I'm a seven-day Advent."

With no preliminaries, Dad had cut right to the core of his morning's discussion. Mom was in shock. She almost dropped the bowl of mashed potatoes in the colporteur's lap. "Martin, don't tell me you wasted your whole morning on religion—to discover that you are a seven-day whatever!" She tried to keep the sharp edge from her voice as she responded in German. She didn't want her guest to know how angry she felt.

"Don't go completely crazy! You read the Bible, come up with all kinds of fang-dangled ideas—even to keeping the Jewish Sabbath. Now you claim to belong to a church that doesn't exist."

"Oh, but it does, Greta! Jack here is an Advent too." Dad's sky-blue eyes sparkled with the delight he felt. "I knew that God must have a church on earth that followed His word. And He does! Jack told me all about it this morning."

"Sure took him long enough," Mom complained under her breath.

"I believe God sent Jack here in answer to my prayers."

"I'll bet!" Mom muttered, not at all certain that God was responsible.

"What is more, Jack has a wonderful book full of Bible lessons. I hope all of our neighbors will buy it too. I'm going to write a letter of recommendation for it. Then I thought, Greta, that you might want to loan him your horse and buggy for the summer. It's hot walking from house to house, carrying a satchel of books."

"How generous of you to offer him my buggy," Mom retorted, still speaking in German which she was sure the colporteur did not understand. "Martin, I just can't believe what has happened to you this past year. What you believe, and what that, that book teaches is, is just Jewish propaganda. Here in America! I thought I escaped that four years ago when I left my homeland to settle in utopia. Already my illusion of that has evaporated, but I had hoped to have a happy home with you. Now this religion thing of yours..."

"All right, Greta," Dad responded calmly in German, sensing at last that Mom was absolutely resistant to his beliefs. "You have the right to feel the way you do. You are so busy with all of your work and the children that you have not had the time to study what I have. I have been amiss in not reading to you. We will discuss this later, but for now I'd like to revert back to talking Danish which we all understand."

Mom was assuaged. Jack's gracious manners and disarming smile made the ladies feel comfortable in his presence. In fact, before the meal was finished, they rather liked Jack in spite of his crazy religion.

For the next few days, Jack canvassed the neighborhood carrying with him Dad's recommendation. Since Dad had a reputation of being quite a Bible scholar, many of the neighbors bought Jack's book. They wanted to know what Martin knew, and they figured this was a shortcut to that knowledge without involving Dad.

On Friday night Jack returned to our house so that he and Dad could keep Sabbath together. Mom and Grandmother were not pleased that Dad left the hay lay in the field over Sabbath. It would probably mold before Monday. It took considerable effort on the part of the ladies to hold their tongues, even though they got some relief by sharing with each other their disapproval of Dad's actions.

Then, of all the irrational things imaginable to do, the men got busy on Sunday morning and hauled in the hay. Now if that didn't smoke Mom's mirror! Whatever would the neighbors think. No one in this Lutheran, Methodist, and Catholic community hayed on Sundays!

Only a few weeks passed, however, before mother's animosity had dissolved, and she let the nice young man borrow her horse and buggy to make his calls and deliver his books. On Friday nights and Sabbaths, Dad and Jack studied the Bible Readings book together in Danish. They pretended to ignore Mom's omnipresence, while she pretended to be busy with household chores within earshot of the study. By the end of the summer, both Dad and Mom were converted. They traveled in the lumber wagon to the

Sioux River where they were baptized, making them the first Adventist family in Moody County.

Jennie arrived December 4 , 1908, to join three-and-a-half-year-old Nels and two-year-old Dorathy. My parents enjoyed their children, farm, and community, but they missed going to church services. Sabbaths were lonely days. Then, in the spring of 1909, Don and Laura Prior, Adventists from North Dakota, moved into the county with their two small sons. That summer, the conference put the two families in touch with one another. If the conference had not, the neighbors would have. After all, anyone "keeping Saturday for Sunday" was so strange that everyone knew about them.

The Priors and the Thompsons met every Sabbath in one home or the other for worship. Dad taught the Sabbath School lesson, and the men took turns reading from the Bible and Mrs. White's books for the church service. The families had dinner together and then split up early enough in the afternoon to return to their farms for chores. Though just five miles separated the farms, it was quite an effort to make the trek during the winter months. But worshipping together was so important to these new Adventists, that no inconvenience or discomfort could keep them from their weekly appointment.

Then Priors had a baby boy, and the Thompsons another girl (Martena, born April 19, 1910). Adding little Sabbath School members was nice, but the Thompsons and Priors wanted other families to join them to form a regular church. They loved the Adventist message and wanted to share it with their neighbors. So Dad wrote to the conference office asking them to send an evangelist to hold a series of meetings in the Kluge School. The conference filled the request by sending Elder Gjording, who spoke Danish, and young Mr. Anderson, who translated into English. Unfortunately, they arrived during the busy harvest season of 1911, and almost no one attended the meetings.

The school board chairman, Charley Scriven, sensed the disappointment of Dad and Don. "I'm what you might call an infidel myself, but if you bring a preacher who speaks English only, I'll promise you an audience. Translating from Danish takes too much time."

So Dad and Don persuaded Mr. Anderson to stay until the harvest was over, then conduct a series of meetings in English. Mr. Anderson agreed to the plan. Charley, true to his word, rounded up an audience. He called on his neighbors, telling them, "If you want to hear a sermon from the Bible, you'd better go to the meetings at the school."

Anderson was an interesting speaker, and people, now that they had time, came out to hear his message. Even Charley, the infidel, feeling somewhat obligated to attend the meetings because of his propaganda, drove his team and wagon every night to the schoolhouse so that Nell and the kids could listen. Then he waited in the hall for them until the meeting was over. Imperceptibly the message was making inroads into Charley's heart, though he wouldn't admit it. When Mr. Anderson left for college, Elder D. P. Miller and his wife took over the interest. They completed the series and in the late fall of 1911 baptized Mr. and Mrs. Godfrey Thompson, Ole, Moody, Kate, Magda, and Chris Thompson (none of these were related to our family), Fern Lewis, Nell Scriven, Vern Martinson, and my grandmother, Dorthea Elenore Thompson. An official Sabbath School and church was organized at the

Kluge School on November 18, 1911. The adults, along with the unbaptized children, made a company of about 30 people.

The Priors and Thompsons were extremely pleased that so many people joined their ranks, but they were not as yet completely satisfied. They were especially anxious for Charley to join the church. But Charley alleged, "Religion is a fine thing for women and children, but I don't need it. I'm willing to take my chances." Whereupon, Miller, hearing this, decided to preach a sermon on the seven last plagues. Even that did not scare Charley into making a decision. At Nell's insistence Charley studied the Bible, but for the wrong reason. He wanted to prove to Martin and Don how foolish they were. But study of the word led to his own conversion. In 1912 Charley was born again through baptism. That same year his son, John, and my brother, Julius, were born, adding more members to the Sabbath School.

Dad hired John Gjording, son of Elder Gjording, to work for him that summer. John was a very intelligent, ambitious young man, but he had not accepted Christ. So Dad flung out his gospel net to capture John for Jesus. Dad expected everyone at our house, including hired hands, to participate in morning and evening worships. John got some good doses of religion during those sessions. Besides that, Dad took every opportunity to drop gems of truth on John. The young man soon yielded to the power of the Holy Spirit.

Meanwhile, Don was sharing his faith with his hired man, Arnie Swartz, and the hired girl, Lela Levee. On September 8, 1912, it was a pleasure for Elder Gjording to return to Colman to baptize his son John, along with Lela and Arnie.

Things were moving fast for the Colman Seventh-day Adventist group. On November 3, 1912, Dad, Charley, Don, and Godfrey met at Chris Thompson's and voted to build their own church with the money that Elder Babcock had previously solicited from the members. Charley donated an acre on the corner of his farm for the church. The very next day the men met on the land and started digging the foundation for the little white church on the hill. The conference sent Elder Rubendahl, an experienced builder, to supervise the project.

While the building took shape, Elder Rubendahl doubled as an evangelist at night, preaching in the Gale Ridge School House. Gus and Alfred Youngberg, public school teachers from Minnesota, and Mrs. Seina Flatten were converted. On May 4, 1913, the same day the church was dedicated, these three people were baptized. Then the enthusiastic Youngberg brothers studied with their sister Ruth.

Dad and Don considered the miracle that had taken place in just two short years. The Adventist membership had grown from four adult members to 25, plus about 25 children—five Scrivens, five Thompsons, seven Flattens, three Priors, and those scattered among the other Thompson families. With half the church being children or youth, the devoted new Adventists determined to train their precious heritage for the Lord. In the fall of 1914 they hired Lela Garrett to teach elementary school in the church and sent the older youth to Plainview Academy. Cord Scriven wasn't fond of completing his senior year at the academy, but he was converted there.

During the next decades many changes took place within the Colman church. The Otters and Simmermans joined; Laura Prior and Nell Scriven died. Children grew and left home for work or school. Their places were filled by new babies. I was among the last to be born into this original, closely-knit church family—only Betty and Harold Flatten (grandchildren of Seina), Thelma Otter, Cleone Simmerman, and Donnie Prior were younger. Lela Levee and Cord Scriven were married, and he became an ordained minister the pride and joy of our church. Alice Flatten married Carl Christensen and they went as missionaries to South America. The three Youngbergs entered the work; Ruth married a minister, and the boys became ministers. Thelma and Ethel Scriven left to take nurse's training. Gladys Flatten and my sisters Jennie and Martena became teachers. But through all of the changes, additions and subtractions, the spirit of love and devotion remained constant.

The consistent spiritual growth of our church family could be traced directly to the leadership of the founding members. As their knowledge of the scriptures increased, so did their faith and their leadership. Our small church never had a full-time pastor, but we really didn't need one. Every member was a priest—guiding, loving, and teaching us children and encouraging one another. They didn't come to church just to see their adult counterparts; they spent time talking to us children. They made us know that we truly were "a heritage of the Lord," that they were praying for us and preparing us to serve in this world and inherit a place in heaven. As soon as we could speak, we were stood up in front to repeat memory verses. Before we could carry a tune, we stood with the older children who could sing properly praising God in song. Before we were teenagers, we participated in the Sabbath School and worship services and held responsible church offices. Then we were given many positive strokes from our church family for doing our jobs well.

The first Sabbath of every month was young people's Sabbath. We presented the entire service with special music, poetry, and message.

Our church parents taught us to test God's promise "to pour out His blessings" through the Investment program. Every spring a big chart was hung on the wall. On it was recorded the name of every Sabbath School member, old and young, naming the project that member had chosen for investment. Mom generally had us invest a setting of hen eggs or a bottle lamb.

One year I invested the black walnuts from one of our trees. The idea seemed brilliant. All summer long I had nothing to do—just watch the tree grow nuts. Then fall came. I had to harvest and crack the nuts. I spent every Sunday cracking nuts and fishing out the meats. My hands remained stained from one week to the next. I supposed they would be a brownish tan color forever. The nuts didn't sell well either. I earned less than half of what my sisters did. The next year I invested a setting of eggs and sold the chickens when they were grown.

Weeks of prayer were special seasons of homemade spiritual emphasis. All of us looked forward to the sleigh rides on those crisp November nights when we could hear the snow crunch under the sleigh's runners and the horses' harnesses jingle jangle. The bright moonlight made the snow sparkle as if blue, gold, and white diamonds had been sprinkled over it. Thus nature itself prepared our minds and hearts for the prompting of the Holy Spirit. We met at a different home every night to read through the message in the Review and Herald. Then we divided into smaller groups for prayer—everyone participated.

The last Sabbath of the week, everyone brought a special Week of Sacrifice offering. Before the week began, our family planned what we would sacrifice to make this offering as large as possible. The sum total of our weekly cash income wasn't enough to satisfy our desire to give. So Dad usually sold an animal and gave the money he received from the sale. This was a sacrifice for our family. We would have to do without something we needed or wanted in order to give this offering. But it felt so good to drop that envelope into the offering plate on Sabbath that we never counted it as much of a sacrifice. I could just imagine that money paying for some missionary's salary or feeding hungry children or caring for the sick heathen. It seemed as if that special offering was dropped right into the hands of God to distribute as He saw best.

The spirit of sacrifice was part of our religion because it was born out of love. And God returned that love in the many ways He blessed us. Our crops never failed. The total amount of giving per capita is staggering. From 1912 to 1922, the Colman Church gave $4,862 in tithe and $4,909 in offerings. (This does not include the cost of building and furnishing a new church, running the church school, etc.) During the next decade 1923-1932, the tithe was $2,949 and the offerings $7,038. (Those offerings include my black walnut Investment project money.) Overall, from the beginning of the Colman Church, the members have consistently given over 20% of their income. So as we children grew, we embraced the same plan of giving practiced by our founders—believing that we too, should live and give to further God's cause.

Every three months we had communion service, a meaningful ritual practiced by all Adventist congregations. Charley Scriven, our head elder, led out. First, we had testimony meeting at which time sins were confessed, wrongs made right, and love for God expressed. I never had anything against anyone to confess, and my sins were too numerous to mention so I took care of them privately with God, but I wanted to declare my love for Jesus publicly. For some reason, I always cried as I tried to express my innermost feelings. I didn't want to cry, but I knew I would, so I always packed some extra hankies in my pocket for communion Sabbath. Then we would have the communion bread and wine, sing a song, and go home. I liked the quarterly service because it made me feel all pure and free from sin again—like a mini-baptism.

Sometimes I wondered if I should confess that I was the culprit in the frog incident at the Friday night youth meeting at Simmermans. I hadn't meant to cause a disturbance, but things went wrong for me, as usual. Lela, Gladys, and I had walked up to the corner of the country road where the Scriven boys would pick us up and take us to the young people's meeting. While we waited, I discovered some cute baby frogs in the road ditch. I caught seven of them and dropped them into my dress pocket, intending to take them home after the meeting and make pets of them. However, once we got to Simmermans, a rousing song service made me forget about the pets in my pocket. During prayer, I leaned forward slightly as I knelt, and my dress pocket gaped open. Before I realized it, the frogs had escaped. When I felt in my pocket, only one slimy fellow remained. I opened my eyes and looked around, knowing I should catch them before the prayer ended. But the frogs had made a quick getaway. I saw none of them. Then Mrs. Simmerman let out a scream, and I knew that one of my frogs was visiting her. Prayer was cut short. "I'm sorry," she said, "I thought it was a mouse that jumped on my foot, but now I see it was only a little frog. There he goes!" While she wondered how the frogs had gotten into her house, the rest of us rounded up four of them. When I dumped the two I had caught outside, I released the one from my pocket too. I worried about the other two frogs but thought it wise not to mention that two more amphibians were still unaccounted for.

Mother taught the children's Sabbath School classes for many years. We met with the adults for the Sabbath School proper and separated only for the lesson study. I learned my memory verses faithfully and treasured the picture cards on which they were written. Then we kids would repeat these scriptural gems for the Thirteenth Sabbath program. The goal of the adults was to train us children for church leadership, and they succeeded. Nearly every child from the Colman Church became local leaders or served the church in some professional capacity.

In my Sabbath School were girls I liked—Wanda Scriven, Betty Flatten, Thelma Otter, and Cleone Simmerman. Then there were the boys I ignored, who sat on the opposite end of our Sabbath School room. It worked real well until the Warner boys came and upset our pattern.

Mrs. Warner's parents were Adventists and came every summer to spend time with their daughter. When they did, they came to our church and brought along Mrs.

Warner and her three sons. Bobby, the oldest, was quite well behaved—almost dignified. But then there was Dick. He always wanted to sit next to me and pull down on my long curls just to watch them snap back up. "Just like bed springs," he observed satisfying his curiosity. If I pushed him away, he pinched me. If I moved, he followed me. He pinched the other girls too. We girls agreed that Dick was doomed for hell and wished it would happen before the sun arose on another Sabbath. Little Gene Warner was too young to know what was going on. He only disturbed the class by falling off his seat, and crying until we wrestled the little guy back up on his chair. We girls were always relieved when the grandparents left so that we would have relief from Dick and Gene.

Mother was quite concerned about my "attitude," and I listened to her sermonette. But secretly, it did not change my mind. Mother thought they were "such a sweet family." Sometimes I wondered about mother's assessment of people, even thought she was usually right. A few years later, Dr. Warner, his wife, and boys joined the church. The Warner boys turned out to be very fine men.

Mother used to bribe me to insure good behavior during the church service. She didn't like the idea of taking kids out and spanking them. (She didn't go for spankings much, just a swift swat on demand.) So between Sabbath School and church she opened her handbag took out a big, round sugar cookie wrapped in wax paper, and tempted me. "Midge, you can go out into the entryway and eat this cookie IF you think you can be quiet during church."

My mouth watered as I eyed the bait. I always thought I could be quiet, and usually was, even if it meant I slept through Elder Stanley's bimonthly sermons or Charley's monthly readings. I didn't like Charley's reading, but I liked Charley. After church he would go to the vestibule to greet the members. He always managed to fish some red-hots out of his pockets and distributed them to us kids. You can bet I didn't dawdle getting out of church

Our church members had such large families that there was only room for the younger children to sit on the pew with their parents. The teenage girls sat sedately on the pew in front of ours. The boys settled for the pew in front of the maidens. That is, all but a few young bucks who isolated themselves in the very back pew. There they desecrated God's house by socializing and whittling with their pocket knives. This concerned Mother because she loved those boys. She felt compelled to speak to their parents.

"Please make your boys sit with you during church. They are practicing irreverence back there. God says we are to reverence His sanctuary. Even Mrs. White says, 'They (the children) are too often found in groups, away from the parents, who should have charge of them.' (5 T, 496) Take steps now to save your boys."

"But teenagers are a difficult age," some parents argued to excuse themselves.

"So were Eli's sons. Smack dab in the middle of church, officiating. And you know what happened to them and the bad influence they had upon the other members," Mom responded pointedly but kindly.

For a brief time the parents made feeble attempts to retrench and retrieve their sons. But when they met with resistance, they gave up their parental responsibilities. So though it broke their hearts, the church family watched most of those boys turn their backs upon God.

Mother called the back pew "Devil's Row," and you can bet that neither Nels or Julius dared sit there. After Nell died, Charley was left to raise the three younger boys by himself. Poor Charley! He was doing his best, but the twins were always one step ahead of him. When Wayne and Ward took to sitting on Devil's Row instead of with my brother Julius, their brother John, and the Otter boys, Mom cornered Charley. "Nell would never approve of the twins sitting on Devil's Row, fooling around during church service. Charley, you had better make those boys sit up with Julius and John or they will develop bad worship practices. I know you want them to respect the sacredness of the church and God. Nell will expect to see those boys in heaven. It's all up to you now, since she's gone. Please do something about it."

I don't know what Charley did, but the twins moved from Devil's Row, though they still made a few detours into the devil's territory during the week. But the training and example of Charley and our church members eventually paid off—the twins both became ministers.

About the time I learned to enjoy Charley's messages, Donnie Prior was born. Some years after Laura's death, Don had remarried. Eva, his second wife, was a delightful lady, and I liked her a lot. She let me hold the baby after church. I would have liked for Charley's messages to be shorter and my baby-holding period longer, but regulating time was not one of my prerogatives. I was sorry when baby Donnie grew too big to hold and asserted his independence. One day when he was about three, I watched Eva try her best to keep spirited little Donnie quiet. When she went to play the organ, Donnie took off for the great outdoors and the summer sun. I was shocked to see a child LEAVE church, and I figured he might end up like those kids on Devil's Row. After church I confided to Mom, "Donnie's going to hell, isn't he?"

Mother drew back in surprise, a frown creasing her brow. "Whatever makes you say a thing like that? Has God asked you to join his staff as a judge? We don't know anything about what is going to happen to anyone until Jesus comes. Donnie's still a little boy, and Eva's not done with him yet."

When Charley or the young people weren't in the pulpit, Elder Stanley from Madison was. His sermons were beyond my comprehension, so I made up stories to entertain myself during church. I usually ran out of story before Elder Stanley ran out of sermon. I thought it would be nice if Elder Stanley would have compensated me for suffering through his long homilies by rewarding me with some red-hots or corn candy. He was one of the few hell-fire and damnation preachers. He appeared to get no pleasure from life. Since every other person in the congregation was a happy Christian, I figured that sternness was just a part of his preacher's oath.

One day after church, Elder Stanley stood in the foyer greeting the people as usual. Grasping my hand tightly, he pulled me close to him and said, "Young lady, pride is swallowing you up."

"Wh—what?" I stammered, too young to catch his metaphor.

"You must rid yourself of pride. Look at you! So young, and already curling your hair to make yourself appear beautiful. Don't you know that God wants only a beautiful heart, not outward adorning? And what does Isaiah 3:16-26 say about jewelry and crimping pins to curl your hair?

173

And Peter, in 1 Peter 3:3, condemns the plaiting of hair and the wearing of gold. God can't take you to heaven like this."

I was stunned. I had no idea what Stanley, Isaiah, or Peter was talking about—pride, crimping pins, and plaiting hair. Waves of confusion engulfed me. My mouth dropped open, leaving not a muscle strong enough to move my tongue.

Mom came to my rescue. "Now, Elder Stanley, we don't curl Midge's hair. It is naturally curly and because it is damp today, the ringlets are tighter than usual."

"Well, Sister White says it's a sin to curl your hair. You could surely straighten it some to make her look more, ah, more plain. Mrs. White says we shouldn't stimulate pride in our daughters, Sister Thompson."

"That she does. But I don't recall her writing anything about curly hair," Mother responded kindly. Mom led me to the car, and we drove home. But I couldn't forget Elder Stanley's words. As I interpreted them it meant I was going to hell because I had curly hair. I didn't think that was fair of God to give me curly hair and send me to hell for it. And Mom said I wasn't to judge Donnie, so how could Mrs. White judge me? I'd heard such nice things about that lady, but now I didn't like her anymore, even if she was God's messenger. I kept mulling things over in my mind.

At the supper table I blurted out, "Nels, do you know you and I are going to hell?"

"No, I didn't," Nels laughed. "I don't know about you, but I hadn't planned on going to hell at all."

"Well, you will. Elder Stanley said we would because we got curly hair just like Dad. Only I don't suppose Dad will go to hell because his pride is almost gone—he's about bald."

"Yep!" Nels joked, feeding my childish fear. "Well, since we're stuck with curly hair, maybe we'd better invest in some asbestos suits to keep us from burning."

"Nels!" I screamed on the verge of tears. "It isn't funny. I don't want to go to hell—even in an asbestos suit!!"

Nels sobered, realizing that I was as serious as a heart attack. "Don't worry, Midge. We will go to heaven with curly hair. God gave us curly hair, and He won't hold that against us. Elder Stanley is a sincere man, but he's wrong about this point. The Bible doesn't say it's wrong to have curly hair. Jesus was born a Jew, so He probably had curly hair. You've got to read the Bible for yourself. Sometimes people misinterpret what the Bible is trying to say. I've read a lot of Mrs. White's writings. I can't recall a thing she says against curling one's hair. She advises against pride, but not against looking attractive. So don't worry anymore. I'll grab your hand, and we'll fly up to heaven together, and God will pat our curly heads."

Nels was so comforting that I ran to his chair and kissed him. "Let's not get too mushy, now," he warned, giving me a bear hug.

"Then all of the Colman church people will be able to know us in heaven?" I concluded, rubbing a finger gently against his cheek.

"That's right. And I expect most of them, along with Elder Stanley, will be there. Isn't that exciting?"

It was exciting, indeed. Almost too exciting for sleep to overtake me when I got to bed. I dreamed of my church family in heaven, living close together so I could play with Wanda, Betty, Thelma, and Cleone. If the Warner boys got there, God would make them real nice, and Dick wouldn't pull my curls. I might even ride lions with the Otter and Flatten boys. Surely Ida Otter and Joanna Simmerman would play the piano and Charley would have some part in the worship services. Mom, of course, would help the angels teach us children our Sabbath School lessons. And Eva, even as she gripped Donnie's hand, would say nice things to everybody. My sisters, along with Laura, Grace, June, and others would join the choir. Heaven was just the place for my family from the little white church on the hill to enjoy eternity.

Chapter 18

The New Dress that was Hardly Worn

I was thrilled with the new dress Mother was sewing for me. I would wear it to the church's Fourth of July picnic just one week away. I prided myself on the selection of material—pink flowers with yellow centers on a white background. I believed the style I had combined to be the best—butterfly sleeves, two-tier gathered skirt, and a triangular neckline. Maybe it was a bit outlandish, but an 11-year-old girl can get caught up with the need to be fancy. Then I watched eagerly as Mom measured, cut, and sewed my dream dress.

"I'm about ready to fit it on you," Mom announced, looking up at me with a smile. But before I could slip into the soft wonder, the telephone rang. I ran to answer it.

"Mom, it's Wanda. She wants to come over and pick me up. We'll ride her horse over to Nels and Ethel's place. Old Billy (I used 'old' intentionally to disarm Mom of objections) is such a gentle horse. We ride him all over when I go to Scrivens. (Whoops! I let the cat out of the bag, but Mom didn't seem to notice.) May I go?"

"Yes, I suppose. But first, let's get this dress fitted and the hem pinned up. I still have to make Gladys' and Lela's dresses."

I relayed the confirmation to Wanda suggesting that we make a picnic of the excursion. She thought it was a "scathingly brilliant idea."

Mom handed me the new dress and I slipped into it. I ran to the mirror to see what it looked like on me. Ah, I liked what I saw. I turned this way and that, feeling for all the world like a fairy princess.

"Come here, Midge," Mom commanded in her no-nonsense voice. "Hmmm, it seems to fit okay, but—dear me! You've grown more than I thought. This dress is almost too short. Hmmm! I can't even make a hem just roll it under. You'll have to wear it a lot this summer to get the good out of it. You can take it off now, Midge."

I danced across the room, swishing and swirling to make the skirt balloon out. I could just imagine the compliments I would get on the dress when I wore it to the Fourth of July picnic. Wanda and Betty would not be envious, but they would admire it sufficiently to satisfy my ego.

"Take the dress off NOW, Midge. I don't have time to fool around. Honestly, you act as if you are Cinderella going to the ball," Mom fussed.

I wanted to answer, "Honestly, I feel just like that." But I kept my thoughts to myself and pulled the dress over my head. I laid the dress down gently on Mom's Singer sewing machine and gave it a final caress. "Thanks, Mom, for doing such a perfect job."

While I waited for Wanda to ride Billy the two miles to our house, I made some peanut butter and raisin sandwiches and wrapped them in wax paper. Then I snatched a few gingersnap cookies and tossed the lot into a paper bag.

As the screen door slammed shut behind me, I called over my shoulder, "Bye, Mom. See ya' in time for chores." Then I ran down to the end of the lane to wait for Wanda. I didn't have long to wait. Wanda urged Billy over to where I was balancing precariously on the top of a wooden fence post. When Billy was close enough, I launched myself onto his back. I settled myself comfortably behind Wanda, and we were off. We farm kids always rode bareback. We couldn't afford saddles, and we didn't think to use blankets either. We were so pleased to have transportation that we didn't even notice the horse's coarse, prickly hair.

We talked excitedly as Billy trotted off down the dusty country road. We hadn't gone a fraction of a mile before we decided it was too hot to hurry. "Hey, Wanda, let's stop by the creek and eat our sandwiches under the willow trees. It's about noon, and I'm hungry."

"So am I. Billy can eat grass and drink from the creek while we eat."

"Oh no! I forgot to bring something for us to drink!" I exclaimed.

"Well, we'll just have to do without," Wanda said, settling herself comfortably on a tree stump. "We surely can't risk drinking creek water—there's so much stomach flu going around. I wouldn't want to get sick just before the church picnic."

"Neither would I!" I agreed, handing her a sandwich. It took a lot of saliva to down the peanut butter and raisin sandwiches without some liquid, but we had the time. While we ate, I wedged into the conversation a description of my new dress. Then we planned activities we would enjoy at the picnic: a ball game in which all able bodies would participate, a horseshoe pitch, a three-legged race,

179

etc. We'd try to get out of cranking the freezers, but we'd lick up several bowls full of homemade ice cream. The men usually considered cranking the freezers their contribution to the feast, anyway, so we never really needed to concern ourselves with that. But it made fun conversation. When we finished our lunch, we led Billy over to a tree limb and dropped down on his back.

Soon we came to the corner where Nels' pasture began. "Look, Wanda, there are Nels' cattle and that dumb old Rosie."

"You really don't like that horse, do you, Midge?" "And for good reasons. Just before Nels took her over

to his place, Lela tried to ride her. Lazy Rosie objected, of course, but Lela finally got on her. The first thing Rosie did was to walk right over to the apple tree, rub against the trunk, and scrape Lela right off. Then Rosie slipped her bridle and galloped off to the pasture. Gladys and I picked Lela up off the ground. Her leg was all scratched and bleeding and filled with chips of tree bark."

"Boy, she is ornery!" Wanda conceded.

"Meanest hunk of horse flesh this side of the wild west rodeos. We girls can't ride her, just Nels and Julius. BUT a few weeks ago I was dumb enough to try it once more. I had come home from church with Nels and Ethel. (Colman had services in the afternoon.) I wanted to help Nels with the chores so I offered to ride Rosie down to get the cows. Nels was reluctant to let me, because he didn't think I could keep her from slipping her bridle and leaving me down in the pasture with that old white bull, Orphan Fairfax."

"Oh, I know the bull you mean," Wanda said. "Uncle Charley was afraid he'd kill someone before your dad could sell him at the stock-yards."

"That's the very one. Well, I promised Nels I'd keep the reins tight, and he hoisted me onto her back. Rosie and I were off. I thought we were getting along famously. We rounded up the milk cows and headed them down the lane. Rosie had behaved so well I thought I would treat her. I let her head down just a little so she could nibble on some juicy grass. And, don't you know it? She slipped her bridle, reared up, and dumped me off her rear. There was Orphan Fairfax pawing up the real estate. Rosie took off for home, and SO DID I. Rosie galloped up behind the cattle, but they were so tightly bunched together in the narrow lane that she couldn't get around them. She scared the cattle into a stampede. She ate their dust, and I made quite a meal of it too. The cattle and Rosie beat me home—but not by much!"

Wanda laughed so hard she nearly fell off Billy. "Wanda," I chided, "it wasn't funny! I could have been trampled to death by that bull. I'll tell you Nels was happy to see my dusty face."

"I know. I know!" Wanda agreed, still chortling some. "I can just imagine what a funny sight the lot of you must have made, racing up that quarter of a mile lane. There was probably so much dust that Orphan Fairfax lost sight of what he was chasing." Wanda mopped her eyes on her shirt sleeve.

I was slightly ruffled that anyone could find humor in my terrifying ordeal, but by this time we had reached Nels and Ethel's driveway. We hopped off Billy, tied him to a post, and ran for the house.

"Water! Water!" We pleaded like wayfarers from the desert.

Ethel ladled water into our glasses from the bucket by the kitchen sink. "You girls must really be thirsty," she commented. "You camels have emptied the pail. Now if you'll go pump some cool water from the well into the bucket, I'll make some nectarade to help wash down some of this fresh cake."

Our mouths watered as we watched Ethel finish swathing the three-layer caramel cake with fluffy frosting. We knew we could polish off a piece or two of that. In a flash we were off to the well.

Nels came in for lunch, and the four of us sat around the kitchen table drinking nectarade and eating that scrumptious cake. Wanda scraped the last bit of frosting off her plate just like I did—after our second piece.

The afternoon passed quickly away. It was late when Wanda and I jumped back on Billy and started for home. At the end of my driveway, I slipped off Billy, told Wanda I'd see her Sabbath, and hurried to do my chores. For some reason, I wasn't feeling quite right. At the supper table I excused my disinterest in food by saying, "Guess I ate too much of Ethel's delicious cake."

"Well, it was also a hot day, and you're probably just too tired to eat," Mom reasoned. "While your sisters clear the table, take your bath and get to bed early."

I was grateful for the excuse to bathe and hop into bed. Later, Lela crawled into the double bed with me (we always slept together), and Gladys into her single bed, but I was still awake. I tossed and turned the whole night, only sleeping intermittently. The next morning I couldn't drag myself out of bed. My whole abdomen was distressfully painful and getting worse by the hour.

"Come on, Midge," Gladys called impatiently. "Get out of bed and help with the Friday's cleaning and cooking before it gets so hot."

"Gladys, I can't! I feel terrible," I groaned, pressing the sheet against my eyes to stop my tears. Just about then I began vomiting, giving her satisfactory proof of my claim.

When Mom got Gladys' report, she came up to see me. "Where do you hurt?" she asked, feeling my forehead.

"Ooooh, all over my tummy."

"It isn't in just one spot, like your right side, is it?" Mom questioned as she pressed on my abdomen.

"No, ouch! Oh, don't touch my tummy."

"But I need to find out where it hurts. Last year when Gladys got appendicitis, she had pain in her right side. If it's that, you'll have to have surgery for it. We don't want take any risks."

"No, Mom, it just hurts all over. Just a tummyache. I'll be okay tomorrow."

"Well, all right then. But we'll keep checking on you. I'll send Gladys up with a bell that you can ring, just in case you need help." Mom's very presence was comforting.

As the day wore on, my misery increased. About four in the afternoon, Mom called the doctor to come and look at me, but he was busy delivering a baby in another part of the county. He was the same doctor who had delivered me six months after he had mistakenly diagnosed me as Mom's tumor. By five in the evening, it was raining so badly that it was doubtful that anyone could get anywhere.

Dad came in and looked at me, curled up in the fetal position—the only way I could seemingly get any relief.

"Middy, you are more sick than you are admitting. I'm going to hitch up the horses and go over and get Thelma Scriven. She's a good nurse, and maybe she can give you some relief until the doctor comes," Dad said. He understood me pretty well. Because of my parents devotion to work and their attitude that sickness was akin to one of the seven deadly sins, none of us in the family admitted pain unless we couldn't hide it. I had reached that point.

Thelma, who was Charley's oldest daughter, Ethel's sister, and Wanda's cousin, came the two miles to our house by horse and wagon. She examined me. Since it was now impossible for a car to navigate the muddy country roads, she called the doctor and told him my symptoms. During their consultation, they agreed that I probably had a bad case of the stomach flu and that some hot fomentations might alleviate some of the pain. Mom had already "cleansed me" with her standard remedy—a glass of lukewarm soda water. It made me vomit up everything; probably even the lining of my stomach slipped out with it.

Thelma applied hot fomentations on my stomach (just as she had to my mastoid when I was seven). Halfway through the procedure, something in my abdomen seemed to pop, and I began to feel relief. An hour later she called the doctor and told him that I was resting more comfortably. Both were satisfied that they had effected a cure. Thelma went back home, and I slept. Towards morning I was restless again. I didn't have as much pain in my abdomen, but my legs and arms ached and were swelling. I wondered what could cause that but decided not to bother Mom with that development until morning. So I smothered my sobs and endured the pain.

"A happy Sabbath to you, Midge," Mom called cheerily as she entered my room. "How's my girl today?" I could tell by her optimistic spirit that she expected me to be well.

I couldn't hide my concern. "Oh, I'm stiff and sore all over. Why?" "Hmm. You did toss and turn a lot yesterday. Or you may still be stiff and sore from riding the horse on Thursday. I don't know why."

"Of course. I hadn't thought of that," I said, relieved to hear an explanation.

The family ate their usual Sabbath morning breakfast of cornflakes, iced cinnamon rolls, and hot chocolate. I always looked forward to Mom's special Sabbath meals, but I couldn't even think of looking at a homemade roll that morning. Lela and Gladys gathered wild flowers for my room and read to me. After lunch, the rest of the family went to Sabbath School, which began at 2 p.m. Mom stayed home with me.

After church, Nels and Ethel dropped by to see me. By then I had started running a fever, and my whole body ached. I kept down water and dozed. Ethel, who was also a nurse, was not pleased with my condition. "Something is still wrong with her; if she isn't better by morning, call another doctor."

I passed Saturday night fitfully. I was in and out of sleep, but always in pain. By Sunday morning my arms and legs were very swollen and my abdomen was bloated. Dad and Mom were definitely alarmed and called Dr. Grove in Dell Rapids to come to see me. It had rained again, so Dad met the doctor at the end of pavement with a team of horses and pulled his car through the mud holes the last mile and a half to our house.

Dr. Grove walked into the room, gave me only a cursory examination, and motioned the family out to the dining room. "She has ruptured appendix. Judging from the swelling and all, it has been ruptured for 36 hours or more. We have no medication to combat the poisons in her system. I believe her case is hopeless."

"But can't you do something?" Dad pleaded, tears filling his eyes.

"Not really. We can't operate on her because the toxins have already bloated her body and given her a high fever. She's hardly conscious. The only thing we could do, Martin, is to take her to the hospital and give her morphine injections to relieve her misery until..." the doctor's voice trailed off.

"Well, let's do something, ANYTHING to help my little girl," Dad said in desperation.

Carefully they carried me through the house. As they did so I caught a glimpse of my new dress, pressed and hanging on the living room door, just waiting to be worn to the Fourth of July church picnic. I remembered what I really wanted. "When will I wear my new dress?" I mumbled through swollen lips.

This sent my sisters into another flood of tears. Mother finally rallied to the occasion, "As soon as you are well."

Dad laid me gently on the back seat of the doctor's car, and the horses pulled us back to the pavement. Mother sat with the doctor on the front seat, holding her hurriedly packed satchel on her lap. Every jolt or bump gave me excruciating pain and I drifted in and out of consciousness. I heard mother telling the doctor, "We never imagined she had appendicitis. The pain wasn't ever on her right side. Dr. Doty thought it was the stomach flu too."

"Now, don't blame yourselves or Dr. Doty for the misdiagnosis. These things happen. Sometimes people's appendix give a referred pain throughout the abdomen. This is what happened to Mildred. We might have caught it in the hospital with a blood count. We'll just have to do our best now. Prayer is really the only answer."

"Ours IS a praying family, Dr. Grove, and we have dedicated all of our children to the Lord," Mom explained. "Midge, ah, Mildred, was our bonus child, born after I had ceased with the, the, ah, manner of women. Dr. Doty wanted me to come down to you then and have the 'tumor' removed. The tumor was Midge. And we have enjoyed her—most of the time." Mother had to be honest. "And she wants to be a missionary."

"The mission fields may have to look for another candidate, Mrs. Thompson," Dr. Grove cautioned. "I don't want you to hope, for one moment, that we are going to perform a miracle. And that is exactly what it would take."

"I believe in miracles," Mom said simply.

"Well, may God bless you and reward your faith, but I'd prefer you just accept medical facts. I have told you what they are."

Sunday, Monday, and Tuesday passed. I was still alive, though unaware of anything. The church had their Fourth of July picnic. I was not there wearing my new dress. There was little celebrating; the church and my family spent much time in prayer. But family prayer sessions weren't enough for Gladys. So she did her praying up in the grove of trees where we had made our playhouses when we were younger.

Nels' bride, Ethel, came to the hospital to be my private nurse and support Mom. The two were on duty around the clock. The rest of the family drove the 15 miles to Dell Rapids at least once a day to see me. There were many other visitors too, including my sister Jean and her son Jimmy from western South Dakota. Sister Dorathy came up from Sioux Falls bringing me a beautiful doll, and cousin Leo brought me a set of china dalmatian dogs. Ordinarily all of these things would have stirred up a tizzy of excitement in me, but I had now lapsed into a coma and was unable to enjoy their gifts of love. People in the community began saying, "The Katzenjammer Kid will be sorely missed."

By Wednesday morning, I no longer needed morphine, so deep was my unconsciousness. That morning, after Dr. Grove examined me he turned to Mother, "Mrs. Thompson," he said, "we can't understand how Mildred has lasted so long, but she is bloated so much now, that we need to operate on her to release the gases and poisons in her abdomen before she explodes. We can at least put in drainage tubes and maybe that will give her temporary relief, but that won't take care of the basic problem. Would you and your husband sign this paper allowing us to do this surgical procedure?"

I awakened just briefly in the operating room. They held a mask over my face and told me to breath deeply. I have no idea if I cooperated, but I was too weak to fight it. I do know that the ether made me hear buzz saws, then enter a long tunnel with a bright light at the end. Ether was a terrible, sickening anesthetic, but it was the best they had in those days. I suppose everyone who took it had the same responses as I did—buzz saws, tunnel, bright light, and then nothing.

In reality, there was no bright light at the end of my tunnel. The doctors opened my abdomen and discovered it was filled with gangrene. The stench was so strong that they opened the windows, disregarding all sterile procedures. Ethel, the two doctors, and other nurses claimed they had never seen or smelled anything like it. Initially, Dr. Grove was inclined to just put in drainage tubes and sew me up. But then, he decided to remove the appendix and eight inches of the rotting intestine. He soon regretted that move because he couldn't sew the two cut ends together—the flesh was like wet noodles and wouldn't hold. Besides, my stomach and intestines were all perforated with specks of gangrene. Finally, the other doctor said, "Grove, give up. It's been three hours, and there is nothing you can do. Let's put in the tubes and sew her up."

Dr. Grove agreed, and attempted to sew me up. But the flesh around the incision tore. Finally, he put heavy gauze padding across my abdomen to absorb the seepage from two of the tubes, pulled it as tight as he could and taped it to my sides.

They wheeled me back into my room where Mom was waiting. "Mrs. Thompson, when I explain to you what we found, then you will know that all hope is gone." I heard that and then drifted off again. Next I heard, "She will probably not come out from the anesthetic. We can hope she will not. I trust you have made funeral arrangements as I suggested earlier. We have placed a heavy rubber sheet under her so that the undertakers can move her without running the risk of becoming contaminated with the gangrene. It is just dripping out everywhere. We just couldn't contain it." I could hear Ethel and Mom crying softly. "I'm sorry," Dr. Grove continued, obviously grieved too. "But it just is not to be. She would have died three days ago if she didn't have such a strong consti…"

"I'm … not … going … to … die," I murmured through parched lips. "Not if Jesus … doesn't … want me to."

Conversation in the room stopped abruptly. "Did, did sh—she say that?" Dr. Grove asked in alarm.

"She's waking up," the shocked nurse mumbled. "I, I can't believe it!"

Soon Ethel was standing by my bed. She took my hand and whispered, "Jesus and I are here with you, Midge." She didn't make any promises of recovery, just comforting words of love and care.

Then I started retching from the effects of the ether. That kept me busy for the next few hours and on the verge of wakefulness.

The next day I noticed two large needles in my legs which were feeding some kind of solution into me. On the side of my bed was fastened a bottle into which one of my drainage tubes fed a greenish, thickish, sickening liquid. Everyone entering my room wore a mask or held a hanky over his nose to filter out the foul smell from the drainage. Visitors stood in the doorway to talk to Mother.

On Sunday some very special people came to my room—doctors from Sioux Falls and other areas. They wanted to see the little girl they had read about in the newspapers. They wanted to verify the stories of the child who had had a ruptured appendix for five days before surgery was performed and was still alive. They wanted to see the intestine preserved in a bottle of formaldehyde and the crinkled-up, black appendix in the other bottle.

"And you couldn't sew the intestines back together?" they asked Dr. Grove again and again.

"That's right. But why should you ask such a question? You are doctors. You know what gangrene does. I don't mean to seem rude, but this whole ordeal has been very stressful on me. Please talk to Ethel Thompson, the nurses, and the other doctor. I knew no one would believe it," Dr. Grove said, sighing wearily.

"Just one more question, please," someone insisted. "You operated on her with a temperature, and her intestines are not fastened together. Is she eating?"

"With a temperature of 103. She's been drinking water. Today we gave her a dip of vanilla ice cream. That's the first food she's had in nine days."

"Well, what will happen to her food with her intestines disconnected?"

"I have no idea. But we had to try food on her sooner or later." "Dr. Grove, how do you explain this medical wonder?"

"I can't explain it, and you can't either. The little girl believed she would live. She believed God would heal her, and who am I to take the credit away from Divine providence? To me it is not a medical wonder. Medicine had nothing to do with her living. Medical science failed, and God took over. I call His recreation a miracle. You can believe whatever you wish. Now, if you will excuse me, I'm going to get some rest. People have been descending on our little hospital like a flock of vultures."

Nine days after surgery, I was given a regular diet. My digestive system worked perfectly. Ethel went home, but faithful Mom stayed on. Even though I was not allowed out of bed, I was my old contented self. I sang happy songs all day long. My room was the first one down from the nurses' station. They left my door open all the time so that the other patients could hear me sing. The patients even sent requests for their favorite songs, and I sang them. Our family had committed to memory many hymns. My doctor had his favorite song too.—"To God be the glory, great things He hath done."

After four weeks, the doctor took out the last drainage tube and gave me permission to leave the hospital. Mom brought down my new dress. I would wear it at last! I had not been out of bed for five weeks, so I sat on the edge of the bed, dangling my feet, as Mom slipped the new dress over my head. Even before I tried to stand to my feet, I knew the dress was far too baggy. My chubby 11-year-old frame had slimmed to a willowy wisp. But I didn't care; I would wear my new dress anyway. When I tried to stand, my legs collapsed. They were too weak to support me. Dad carried me to the car, in my new dress, and our happy family rode home together.

When I finally got my legs to function, I slipped on my new dress again. I looked at myself in the mirror. HORRORS! I must have stretched out several inches. The dress was inappropriately short. I could only wear it around the house. So my new dress was hardly worn. However, I didn't really care about that now; things had lost their value. Life took on a whole new meaning after my brush with death. As I lay on my pillow at night, I would sing in my mind, "Anywhere with Jesus I can safely go," and I wondered just what mission field that would be.

I knew it wouldn't matter because Jesus was making Midge.

Appendix A

Denominational Workers from the Colman Church[1]

Missionaries

John Gjording—minister, missionary to China.

Gus Youngberg—minister, missionary to Borneo. Died in a Japanese internment camp during World War II. Singapore SDA Hospital named for him.

Alfred Youngberg—minister, missionary to India.

Ruth Youngberg Oswald—teacher, missionary to South America.

Alice Flatten Christensen—teacher, missionary to South America.

Grace Flatten Bringle—teacher, missionary to Africa.

Violet Scriven Wittschiebe—teacher, missionary to China, interned in the Philippines during World War II.

Gordon Otter—minister, missionary to Africa.

Lela Thompson Cronk—teacher, missionary to Brazil.

Mildred Thompson Olson—teacher, missionary to the Middle East.

---

1   Almost all of the Colman church members remained faithful and have carried responsibilities in the Adventist churches where they lived. The home mission work they have done has been as important as that done by the church's employed workers. Only space prohibits my mentioning all members of my church family.

Other Denominational Workers

Cord Scriven—minister, president of the North Pacific Union.

Lela Levee Scriven—wife of Cord.

Ward Scriven—minister, conference educational director.

Wayne Scriven—minister, conference Sabbath School and personal ministries director.

Thelma Scriven Barger—nurse, teacher. Ethel Scriven Thompson—nurse.

Jennie Thompson Combes—teacher.

Martena Thompson Bakke—teacher, Portland Adventist Hospital employee.

Gladys Thompson Ring—conference secretary, musician for evangelistic meetings.

Eva Prior—food service director, Plainview Academy.

Donald (Donny) Prior—educator, Andrews University; executive vice president at Glendale Adventist Hospital; vice president of advancement, Loma Linda University.

Lura Simmerman—teacher.

Cleone Simmerman—clinic receptionist. Gladys Otter—teacher.

Bob Warner—teacher, musician. Dick Warner—minister.

Gene Warner—dentist.

Chester Ochenga—food service director, Campion Academy.

Wanda Scriven Ochenga—secretary, Harris Pine Mills, Campion Academy.

DeEtta Knecht Olson—secretary and dean of girls, Milo Academy.

William (Billy) Neptune—minister.

Second Generation Workers Who Were Members Of The Colman Church[2]

Phyllis Scriven Wilburn (daughter of John and Lillian Scriven)—teacher, Newfoundland Conference and Southern Union.

Virginia Scriven Werner (daughter of John and Lillian Scriven)—nurse, Porter Memorial Hospital.

Kathleen Kanzanback Beyrleis (daughter of Ken and Blanch Kanzanback)—teacher, Lake Union.

Janie Kanzanback Titus (daughter of Ken and Blanch Kanzanback)—nurse, Hinsdale Hospital.

Doris Thompson Bacon (daughter of Nels and Ethel Thompson)—teacher, Mid-America Union.

Twyla Ochenga Preston (daughter of Chester and Wanda Ochenga)—teacher, Mid-America.

Robert Ochenga (son of Chester and Wanda Ochenga)—academy food service director.

---

2   Many children of the workers above have become missionaries or are denominationally employed workers. I have not listed any of them since they were never members of the Colman Church.